RESIDENTIAL GEOTHERMAL SYSTEMS

RESIDENTIAL GEOTHERMAL SYSTEMS

Heating And Cooling Using The Ground Below

John Stojanowski

Pangea Publications, LLC
Staten Island, New York

ISBN: 978-0-9819221-1-9

Library of Congress Control Number: 2010924079

Graphics created with CoPlot

10 9 8 7 6 5 4 3 2 1

CONTENTS

About This Book

The words "geothermal energy" usually conjures up the image of steam that is emanating from hot springs in a place like Yellowstone National Park in the western USA. In this region and other places around the world, molten lava resides near the Earth's surface and has been used to produce steam to power turbines to produce electricity.

The average person is not aware that almost any underground location can be used as a source of heat in the winter as well as a place to absorb summer heat from a residence. Residential systems that perform this function have been around for quite some time and are slowly replacing fossil fuel based heating and cooling systems. The primary component of these systems is a heat pump, so named because it transfers or moves heat from one place to another rather than generating heat from some form of combustion.

Why would a homeowner install a geothermal heating and cooling system instead of a conventional one? Although environmental consciousness is one reason, the potential for lower long-term heating and cooling expenses is the primary motivation. This cost reduction is possible because geothermal heating and cooling systems can operate at efficiencies in the 200% to 500% range compared to the best fossil fuel burning systems that operate at 95% to 99%.

The number of residential geothermal systems is small compared to conventional systems, and therefore, the number of experienced installers of these systems is also small. This fact shifts part of the burden of responsibility for the proper design and installation of a geothermal system on to the homeowner. Becoming knowledgeable about the fundamentals of residential geothermal systems will help the homeowner to be in a comfortable position to select a contractor/installer and to work with him to install the best system.

This book provides the homeowner with a considerable amount of information about all aspects of residential geothermal systems. Some of the material may seem technical at times but the more the homeowner learns about these systems, the better the outcome will be for him if he decides to "go Geo."

8

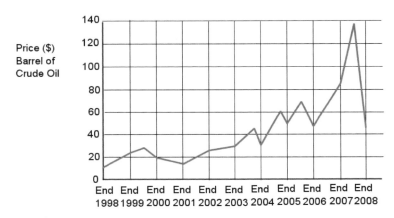

10 YEAR CHANGE IN PRICE OF BARREL OF CRUDE OIL

CHAPTER 1 THE COLD FACTS

1.1 FUTURE SHOCK

It is January 2009 as this is being written. The temperature in New York City is expected to drop to about 5 degrees F. tonight. This temperature is unusually cold for this region and the local news media has given its full attention to this subject. A cartoon in one of today's newspapers depicts Al Gore holding a sign stating "*STOP GLOBAL WARMING*" while he is surrounded by a group of irate, ice-laden, baseball bat carrying protestors. While there is little doubt about the reality of global warming, current homeowners should, if the past is any indication of the future, expect to spend an increasing percentage of their income to heat their homes.

The graph on the facing page displays the year-end price of crude oil for the ten-year period of 1998 to 2008. The steep, post-2006 increase is apparent with a rise of roughly $100/barrel to a peak of $140/barrel. The precipitous drop in price beginning in mid-2008, an indirect result of the home mortgage debacle can be seen. Some would label the rise as a "bubble", one that was not exclusively attributable to the laws of supply and demand but influenced by financial speculators. To the average homeowner, the cause of the rise in oil and other fuel prices is less important than the economic effect it has on them.

Will fuel prices reach those high levels again? I believe they will because the same forces which raised them to their elevated levels will not disappear; they will return when the world economy recovers. Whether a return to full manufacturing productivity in China, India, Southeast Asia and newer centers of low cost employment and/or financial speculation, fuel prices will undoubtedly rise again. How does the average homeowner cope with this eventuality? There is only one solution for those who do not possess exorbitant financial resources. The solution is to use less non-renewable fuel including oil, electricity from the grid, natural gas, propane, coal, wood (if it has to be bought), etc., to heat (and cool) their homes. The price of those fuels will continue to rise in the future.

There is an initial, low-cost step that most homeowners can and should undertake before all others. That is to increase the thermal insulation within their home. This should be the first step undertaken because there will be a benefit regardless of the energy source of heating and cooling.

Figure 1.2.1

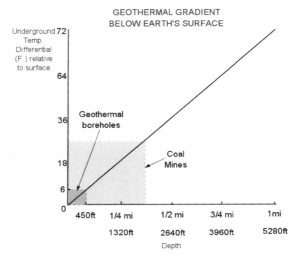

Figure 1.2.2

Collosal Cave, Tucson Arizona	70F.	Onondaga Cave, Missouri	57F.
Laurel Caverns, Pennsylvania	50F.	Jewell Cave, South Dakota	42F.
Wind Cave, South Dakota	53F.	Mammoth Cave, Kentucky	54F.
Marengo Cave, Indiana	52F.		

Figure 1.2.3

USA Map
Mean Earth Temperatures

1.2 THE FURNACE BELOW

Early Stone Age people were aware of the benefit of geothermal energy. The Neanderthal, Cro-Magnon and our more recent ancestors relied heavily on caves as their habitat. Anthropologists have excavated layer upon layer of cave floors revealing continuous use by multiple generations of Paleolithic families. The temperature moderating effects within the caves provided ideal places to inhabit.

One has to wonder if the early northern migration to Europe from Africa would have taken place if early man, acclimated to a warm tropical climate, didn't have caves available to them. It is well known that caves beneath the Earth's surface have temperatures that are nearly constant year round and much more moderate than that at the surface. In fact, the temperature within a cave is approximately that of the average annual surface temperature near the location of the cave. The average annual temperature is computed by summing the average daily temperature for each day of the year and dividing by 365. Figure 1.2.2 lists the underground temperatures of various caves in the United States.

In recent years, earth-sheltered homes have attracted increasing attention. Not only does this type of structure have a natural, aesthetic impact but results in a reduction of fossil fuel usage by 60-85%, according to the proponents. This reduction of fuel usage is, of course, made possible by subsurface, geothermal energy. Most people do not have the resources to design and build a custom, earth-sheltered home, which often requires a sloping terrain. However, geothermal heating/cooling systems can be implemented for most new, as well as existing residences.

The Earth's inner core is primarily made up of a solid sphere of iron within a larger sphere of molten iron. Scientists believe that the reason the core has not lost its high temperature (of 7000 degrees Fahrenheit) is that radioactive decay of uranium and a few other elements within the core continues to this day, after four and one half billion years, to generate enormous amounts of heat. This centralized heat furnace produces a spherical temperature gradient with maximum temperature at the core and diminishing temperatures radially toward the surface. Coal miners can vouch for the excessively high temperature, relatively speaking, several hundred feet below the surface of the Earth. At the depth of these mines the geothermal gradient is approximately 25-30 degrees C./km (or about 15 degrees F. for each 1000 ft increase in depth). Figure 1.2.1 displays the geothermal gradient up to a mile below the surface of the Earth. As shown, for residential geothermal boreholes, an increase of about 6 degrees F. is found at the bottom of the wells that are about 450 feet deep.

Temperatures nearer the surface are more influenced by the Sun's solar radiation and the ambient atmospheric temperature rather than the internal heat source coming from the Earth's central core. The exception to this is when hot springs or magmatic intrusions (i.e., lava flows) are nearby. The effectiveness of geothermal heating/cooling systems which are used to extract heat from the earth just below the surface for use in residential applications, is directly affected by the geographic location. Fig. 1.2.3 displays the average annual ground temperature throughout the continental United States. A more detailed, worldwide list can be found in *Appendix A*. Although it is frequently stated that the undisturbed underground temperature is a constant 55 degrees F. about 6 feet below the surface, a more accurate statement would be that it ranges from about 42 in St. Paul, Minnesota to about 70 in Tucson, Arizona (in the USA).

When it comes to geothermal energy, the purists claim that the term "geothermal energy" should only be applied to the subsurface thermal energy contained in hot springs and magmatic intrusions. There are many of these areas throughout the world, mostly situated along the edges of tectonic plates where volcanic activity supplies vast amounts of heat to depths which can be reached by drilling. There are several ways that thermal energy can be extracted from these areas, including:

a. **Direct Hot Water**- using hot water from shallow depths.
b. **Binary Vapor Flash**- using hot water from deep wells to provide heat to a second fluid with a boiling point below that of water causing it to flash-vaporize. This secondary vapor is used to power an electric turbine.
c. **Direct Steam**- uses the steam produced naturally to power electric turbines.
d. **Enhanced**- uses water from the surface, which is injected into deep wells where it turns to hot water/steam and is recovered from a second borehole to power electric turbines.

Iceland, for example, lies atop the junction between the North American tectonic plate and the European plate. The movement of the plates against each other results in production of volcanic magma below the surface. In many places the resulting steam can be seen drifting from the crevices in the ground. Close to 90% of the homes in Iceland are heated by this volcanic-source type of geothermal energy.

In this book, I will ignore the advice of the purists and use the term "geothermal energy" to also describe an alternate method used to extract heat from subsurface locations. After all, the prefix "geo" is derived from the Greek language and corresponds to the word "earth" and "thermos" corresponds to the word "heat." Accordingly, this book will describe the extraction of heat from subsurface locations below most regions of the Earth, not those that are exclusively dependent on volcanic (magmatic) provinces. And, in these regions, unlike the magmatic provinces, heat can not only be extracted from the ground for heating but can be injected into the ground to provide cooling of a residence.

1.3 GEOTHERMAL....THE SYNONYMS

In order to reduce any confusion that might arise concerning the many names ascribed to the extraction/injection of heat from/into the subsurface depths of up to approximately 450 feet, excluding magmatic areas, a list of commonly used terms to describe this technology is in order. The following is a list of some of these terms:

1. Ground Source Heat Pump (**GSHP**), probably the most common terminology.
2. Geo-Exchange system (**GX**)
3. Water Source Heat Pump (**WSHP**)
4. Earth-coupled system
5. Ground Heat Pump (**GHP**)
6. Ground Coupled Heat Pump (**GCHP**)
7. Ground Source Heat Exchange (**GSHX**)
6. Direct Exchange system (**DX**)

1.4 GEOTHERMAL.... THE PLUSES

The average homeowner is not familiar with the concept of geothermal heating/cooling. Being accustomed to burning some kind of fossil fuel to obtain heat, the average homeowner is taken aback by the geothermal concept, which is to "borrow" heat from below the ground at a much reduced cost compared to burning a fuel. Likewise, extracting heat from the home in the summer and "storing" it underground, making separate heating and cooling systems unnecessary, appears to be a revolutionary concept. Yet, these systems have been around for decades. Detailed throughout this book, the advantages and benefits of a geothermal heating/cooling system can be summarized as follows:

1. A system that is primarily a **renewable energy** system. Energy extracted from the earth will be replenished from solar radiation/Earth's core.
2. A primarily **non-polluting energy** source. It has to be noted here that electricity, most likely from the grid and therefore most likely from the burning of fossil fuels, is needed to power the electrical components of any geothermal system. However, relative to most conventional heating/cooling systems, the total non-renewable fuel consumed is a small amount.
3. A **low maintenance** system, primarily because the thermal transfer loops are buried below

the frost line and the other components, in most instances, are located inside protected structures.

A basically **free energy** source, except for the electrical costs incurred to power the electrical components of the system. The future cost of oil, natural gas, electricity and other fuels is unknown but most likely will increase over time. The much higher efficiency of a geothermal system, on the order of 300%-500%, compared to conventional systems makes geothermal a wise, long-term investment.

5. A **single system** that can both heat and cool.

6. A **quiet system**, most owners of geothermal systems aren't even aware when they are running.

7. Not a potential fire or explosion hazard as compared to conventional heating systems that use natural gas, oil, propane, coal or wood. This might result in lower homeowner's insurance premiums.

8. Safer, no carbon monoxide production possible.

9. May be eligible for substantial **income tax credits**. Currently, there is a generous 30% income tax credit (in the USA) for installing a geothermal system. Some local authorities provide additional incentives.

10. May be eligible for **lower electrical rates** from local utility for installing a geothermal system.

11. Will most likely **increase the resale value of property**.

1.5 GEOTHERMAL....THE MINUSES

1. Geothermal heating/cooling systems are slowly becoming popular; it **may not be easy to find the skilled workers** who could install a system properly.

2. The **high initial installation cost** of the system compared to a conventional system. However, the future cost increases of conventional fuels could shorten the payback period considerably. The 30% Federal tax credit makes the cost differential between installing conventional vs. geothermal systems smaller.

3. A higher learning curve for the homeowner compared to a conventional system. Primarily because there are not a great number of highly experienced geothermal installers, the homeowner must do his "homework" so that he will feel comfortable that the system is properly sized and installed. There are no short-cuts here. By purchasing this book, the prospective geothermal system owner has taken one of the first steps needed to prepare for installing a system which will substantially reduce future heating and cooling costs. It is my belief that the cost of conventional fossil fuels will rise dramatically over the next few decades and those who have the foresight to prepare for that eventuality will be rewarded.

1.6 WHAT'S NEXT?.........

The balance of this book will provide the fundamental information that a potential geothermal energy system user would need to make an informed decision concerning the acquisition of such a system.

Chapter 2 GEOTHERMAL...A DIFFERENT ANIMAL details the comparison of a geothermal system to conventional systems. Comparative efficiency, known as COP (Coefficient Of Performance) for geo-systems will be explored.

Chapter 3 BASIC GROUND LOOP SYSTEMS begins with an example of a primitive loop system and progressively adds components that are needed to simulate a modern geothermal system.

Chapter 4 THE REFRIGERATOR describes how to overcome a basic problem of all geothermal systems, which is: How to raise the temperature of a body, or fluid, by moving heat rather than burning a fuel. The common household refrigerator is analyzed.

Chapter 5 THE GEOTHERMAL HEAT PUMP proceeds after analyzing the refrigerator in Chapter 4 to introduce the heart of the geothermal system, the heat pump.

Chapter 6 THE HORIZONTAL GROUND LOOP introduces the horizontal ground loop, the relatively shallow loop system which "borrows" heat from the ground or "loans" it heat.

Chapter 7 THE VERTICAL GROUND LOOP explains how loops can be placed in deep vertical boreholes where temperatures are more stable throughout the year.

Chapter 8 OPEN LOOP SYSTEMS looks at systems that take advantage of nearby bodies of water, primarily wells, to effect heat transfer without closed loops.

Chapter 9 THE STANDING COLUMN WELL (SCW) looks at a hybrid between open and closed loop systems.

Chapter 10 DIRECT EXCHANGE SYSTEMS (DX) introduces a closed loop system that uses copper tubing and refrigerants instead of water and plastic loops.

Chapter 11 MANUAL-J describes the computer-assisted calculation used to properly size a residential geothermal system.

Chapter 12 FINAL STEPS displays a series of flowcharts detailing the steps a homeowner should become familiar with when working with a geothermal designer/contractor.

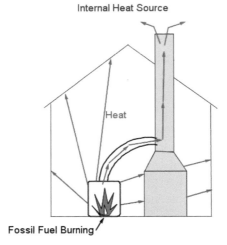

Figure 2.1.1

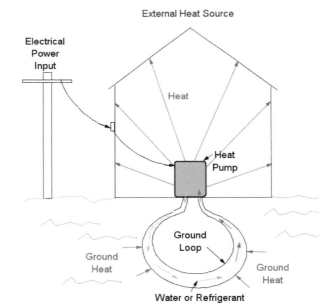

Figure 2.1.2

CHAPTER 2   GEOTHERMAL.....A DIFFERENT ANIMAL

2.1 WHAT'S IT ALL ABOUT?

Since the dawn of civilization, Man has relied primarily on one method of providing warmth to his abode. That method would be the burning of natural substances, beginning with solid fuels, then expanding to liquid and gaseous fuels. It was discovered that the heat content of the various substances varied widely. The following table lists some of these substances and a comparison of their heat producing potential can be made.

Fuel Type	Quantity	Heat Capacity (BTUs)
Residential Fuel Oil	gallon	149,690
Kerosene	gallon	135,000
Natural Gas	therm	100,000
Liquified Petroleum Gas (LPG)	gallon	95,475
Coal	pound	8,100-13,000
Wood	face cord	7,000,000

NOTE: One **BTU** (British Thermal Unit) is the amount of thermal energy, or heat, needed to raise the temperature of one pound of water, one degree Fahrenheit.

In general, to provide heat to an enclosed space, there are basically two methods that can be used:

1. The most common method used is to transform a substance, by way of combustion, into a different, lower energy form. In the transformation process, heat is produced. Figure 2.1.1

illustrates this transformation process taking place within the enclosed space to be heated. Note that some heat is wasted as heated air and smoke vent through the chimney. The result is that 100% heating efficiency is not possible.

2. The other method to provide heat to an enclosed space is to extract thermal energy from an external location and transfer it to the enclosed space without transforming any substance to a different form. This process takes place in just about everyone's kitchen on a daily basis. The common household refrigerator transfers thermal energy from within it to a finned radiator, normally located on the bottom or rear side of the refrigerator which results in the warming of the kitchen. **The common household refrigerator is a heat pump!**

This is the same method of transferring thermal energy used by residential geothermal heating/cooling systems as shown in Figure 2.1.2. These systems are reversible whereby the winter heating function can be reversed in the summer to produce a cooling system. In other words, **unlike conventional separate heating and cooling systems, geothermal systems integrate both functions within the same system.**

Electric power used by the heat pump provides the power to transfer heat from the ground loop to the home's interior. No heat is wasted through a chimney, which is not needed. The efficiency of this type of system, which will be described in detail in the next section, will exceed 100%. In fact, the average annual efficiency of most geothermal heat pump systems will be in the range of 300% to 500%. This startling fact is getting the attention of a lot of cost-conscious homeowners. In addition, there is a generous Federal tax credit of 30% of the installation cost for most residential geothermal systems. This should result in the expansion of **HVAC (Heating, Ventillation, Air Conditioning)** personnel who will become well trained in this relatively new field. It should result in a lowering of the cost of heat pumps as more units are manufactured.

Summary of Internal Revenue Service regulation relative to 30% tax credit (Notice 2009-41)

Section 25D provides a tax credit to individuals for residential energy efficient property. Section 1122 of Division B of the American Recovery and Reinvestment Act of 2009, Pub. L. No. 111-5, amended section 25D for taxable years beginning after December 31, 2008. The amount of a taxpayer's section 25D credit for a taxable year beginning after December 31, 2008, is equal to the following for geothermal systems: **30%** of the **qualified** geothermal heat pump property **expenditures** made by the taxpayer during the taxable year. **Qualified Expenditures.** The expenditures for which the credit for residential energy efficient property is allowed (qualified expenditures) are defined as follows: Qualified geothermal heat pump property expenditures are expenditures for equipment which uses the ground or ground water as a thermal energy source to heat the dwelling unit or as a thermal energy sink to cool the dwelling unit, meets the requirements of the Energy Star program which are in effect at the time that the expenditure for such equipment is actually made (even if under § 25D(e)(8) the expenditure is deemed made at a later time for purposes of determining the taxable year for which a taxpayer may claim the credit), and is installed on or in connection with a **qualifying dwelling unit**. **Qualifying Dwelling Unit.** Except as provided in section 3.01(2)(b) of this notice, a qualifying dwelling unit is a dwelling unit that is located in the United States and is used as a residence by the taxpayer.

 Manufacturer's Certification. In general, the manufacturer of property may certify to a taxpayer that the property meets certain requirements that must be satisfied to claim the credit under §25D by providing the taxpayer with a certification statement that satisfies the requirements of section 3.02(3), (4) and (5) of this notice. The manufacturer may provide the certification statement by including a written copy of the statement with the packaging of the property, in printable form on the manufacturer's website, or in any other manner that will permit the taxpayer to retain the certification statement for tax record keeping purposes. Accordingly, a taxpayer claiming a credit for residential energy efficient property should retain the certification statement as part of the taxpayer's records for purposes of § 1.6001-1(a). In the case of a geothermal heat pump property, the certification should state that the property meets the requirements of the Energy Star program that are in effect at the time that the expenditure for such equipment is actually made.

Content of **Manufacturer's Certification**; Required Declaration. A manufacturer's certification statement must contain a declaration, signed by a person currently authorized to bind the manufacturer in these matters, in the following form: "Under penalties of perjury, I declare that I have examined this certification statement, and to the best of my knowledge and belief, the facts presented are true, correct, and complete."

Labor Costs. Section 25D allows the credit for expenditures for labor costs properly allocable to the onsite preparation, assembly, or original installation of residential energy efficient property described in section 3.01 of this notice and for piping or wiring to interconnect such property to the dwelling unit.

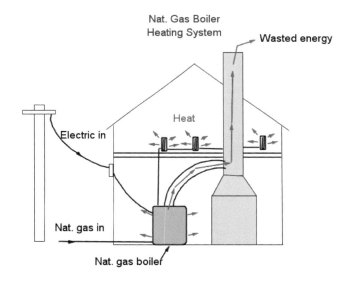

Figure 2.2.1

Nat. Gas Boiler Heating System

Wasted energy

Heat

Electric in

Nat. gas in

Nat. gas boiler

Eff(%)=Total thermal energy delivered to interior X 100

Total input energy needed

=Total thermal energy delivered to radiators and basement X 100

Total energy supplied from Electric and Nat. gas

2.2 Geothermal Heat Pump Efficiency

In a conventional heating system the efficiency is determined by measuring the heat energy (in BTUs) delivered to the structure from the heating unit and dividing that number by the total energy (in BTUs) that was inputted to the heating unit, for some fixed period of time. The illustration of Figure 2.2.1 is that of a residence using a natural gas heating system. It can be seen that the efficiency of this system is:

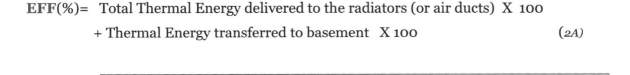

EFF(%)= Total Thermal Energy delivered to the radiators (or air ducts) X 100

+ Thermal Energy transferred to basement   X 100   (2A)

_____

Total Thermal Energy of nat. gas burned + electrical energy to run heating system

From the above definition of efficiency (2A), the efficiency of a conventional heating system must be less than 100% primarily due to the chimney heat loss. Geothermal systems are, in general, 3 to 5 times more efficient than conventional systems. One thing that confuses people is the concept of efficiencies above 100%. They know that their home's natural gas boiler, for example, would be highly efficient at 95% and would be at its theoretical maximum efficiency at 100%, as can be deduced from equation 2A. The efficiency of a geothermal heating/cooling system is generally not expressed as a percentage; an explanation follows.

Geothermal heating/cooling system efficiency is expressed as a **Coefficient Of Performance (COP)** when the system is used in a heating mode and **Energy Efficiency Ratio (EER)** when the system is used in cooling mode. Keeping in mind that geothermal heating/cooling systems are movers of thermal energy rather than creators or transformers, the definition of COP is the ratio of thermal energy delivered by the system (in heating mode) to the total (electrical) energy needed to deliver the thermal energy. This is commonly expressed as:

$$COP = \frac{\text{What You Get}}{\text{What You Pay}} = \frac{\text{Total Heat Delivered to Residence}}{\text{Total Electrical Energy To Run System}} \qquad (2B)$$

As mentioned, geothermal heating systems are much more efficient than conventional systems because they are moving, or transferring, heat from one location to another rather than obtaining heat by transforming (through combustion) one substance into a different form. COP values in the range of 3 to 5 (for heating mode), corresponding to 300%-500% efficiencies, are commonly attained with geothermal systems. Residential geothermal systems are "reversible", meaning they can easily be switched between heating and cooling modes. Although COP usually refers to the heating mode efficiency, sometimes references are made to $COP_{heating}$ and $COP_{cooling}$. Under theoretically ideal conditions, the following relationship can be proven:

$$COP_{heating} = COP_{cooling} + 1 \qquad (2C)$$

The reason why $COP_{heating}$ is greater than $COP_{cooling}$ is because in the heating mode, the energy used to move or transfer the heat to what is called the "hot heat reservoir" contributes to the elevated temperature of that reservoir while in the cooling mode (as in a refrigerator) the energy used to remove the heat from the "cold heat reservoir" does not contribute to cooling that reservoir. From a practical perspective, what this means is the compressor in the heat pump generates heat which is beneficial in the heating mode but is counterproductive when the heat pump is in the cooling mode. The above relationship (2C) helps to explain one reason why HVAC specialists are concerned about having too much heat pump capacity for a geothermal heating/cooling system. If the heat pump for a geothermal system is oversized, or higher than needed, its cooling capacity would be much higher than that needed. If this occurs, then "**short-cycling**", the problematic frequent on/off cycling of the cooling system would occur. As with the a common window air conditioner, if the unit runs only for brief periods, the interior humidity is not sufficiently reduced.

COP, as will be described in *Chapter 5*, is a seasonally variable number for any specific installation. Its value is determined primarily by the temperature of the water entering the heat pump (i.e., the EWT) and the "**uplift**" (the temperature differential between the ground surrounding the loop and the desired interior setpoint temperature). The temperature surrounding the ground loop will vary throughout the seasons. As a matter of fact, COP (for heating) for a specific heat pump will often be specified by the manufacturer for the optimum EWT even though it will vary considerably over the possible range of EWT values. If two identical houses, one in the southern USA and the other in the northern USA, were to install identical systems, the measured COP at any instant in time would be different for the two systems. The main reason for this is the difference in subsurface temperatures of the two locations resulting in different EWTs. In general, the closer the ground loop temperature is to the residence's thermostat setpoint, the higher the COP will be. What the potential geothermal system owner must remember is that heat pump's rated COP, as specified by the manufacturer, is a number obtained under controlled, ideal laboratory conditions. In other words, the "real world" COP that the homeowner will experience will be less than that appearing in the manufacturer's literature. One thing to keep in mind is:

> **COP is independent of fuel costs. As an efficiency measure, it is a comparison of units of energy. To compare the operational cost of running a residential geothermal system versus a conventional system, whether it be a natural gas, oil, propane, etc., system, the cost per unit of fuel must be taken into account.**

2.3 SIZING A RESIDENTIAL GEOTHERMAL SYSTEM (for heating)

In order to design a geothermal system for an existing home, the two functions of heating and cooling must be looked at separately. In general, depending on the geographical location of a residence, either the heating or cooling load becomes the primary consideration when sizing the system. In Florida, USA, for example, the cooling load would be used to size the system and in Michigan, USA, the heating load would be used. In central regions with more moderate temperatures, the loads are closer in size but the heating load is generally used for sizing. The following considerations are for heating only.

The rate of heat loss of any residence, in addition to its physical design characteristics, is affected by the following factors:

1. **The desired interior temperature**. Assuming for the moment that a single thermostat controls the heating system, this would be the winter setting of the thermostat (i.e., the **winter setpoint**). This setting is formally known as the **Winter Inside Design Temperature**.

2. **The outside temperature**. From basic thermodynamics, the rate of heat transfer between two adjacent bodies, in this case the residence and the outside surroundings, is proportional to

the difference in temperature between the two bodies. Of course, wind conditions are also a factor but the assumption being made is that the residence is tightly insulated. Therefore, the lower the thermostat is set, the lower the rate of heat loss for the same outside temperature. The maximum rate of heat loss, or heating load, of a residence cannot be defined until the variables of desired indoor temperature and the expected lowest outdoor temperatures are defined. In order to properly size a heating system it would make sense to first establish the desired winter thermostat setpoint (i.e., the **Winter Inside Design Temperature**) and then use the lowest winter temperatures to determine the maximum heat loss.

HVAC personnel who calculate this heat loss using the two parameters just described do so with a minor adjustment. Instead of using the coldest temperature known for a specific location to determine the heat loss, they select the lowest temperature which will be above the coldest temperatures in that region 97 ½% of the time. This temperature is formally known as the **Winter Outside Design Temperature** and is usually just referred to as the **Winter Design Temperature** or the **Heating Design Temperature**. There are tables from which the Winter Design Temperature can be estimated, called **bin** data, for most cities in the world. *Chapter 11* has an example of this data.

Once the two basic parameters of Winter Inside Design Temperature and the Winter Outside Design Temperature have been established, the geothermal system designer/installer can calculate the **Design Heat Loss**, also known as the **Design Heat Load**, by evaluating the residence design, orientation, etc., using a methodology known as **Manual-J**.

The standard measure for determining quantities of heat (i.e., thermal energy) is the **BTU** (British Thermal Unit), which is defined as the quantity of heat necessary to raise the temperature of one pound of water by one degree Fahrenheit. The Design Heat Loss, which is a rate of heat loss is more commonly referred to simply as the **Heat Load**. Logically, the size of the geothermal system, if it is to totally replace an existing heating system, must be capable of replacing the maximum heat (in BTUs/hour) that is being lost by the residence during the coldest weather. In retro-installations, the older system that is being replaced may be oversized because it was common practice to err on the side of providing too much heating capacity rather than take a chance on installing a system that would leave the homeowner shivering during severe cold spells. Also, the price of heating fuels was much lower in the past. Insulation may have been added since the system was originally installed exacerbating an already oversized-system condition.

How does one estimate the rate of heat loss in a residence? In existing homes, if natural gas is the fuel being used to provide heat, the task is greatly simplified. If the homeowner reads the meter on a daily basis, at the same time-of-day during the coldest periods, preferably on the coldest/windiest days, he will be able to get a fairly accurate estimate of the maximum rate of heat loss (in BTUs/hour). Here's how its done:

1. Record the highest 24 hour usage of natural gas during the winter (normally 1 unit on the natural gas meter is 100 cubic feet of natural gas). Daily recording of the meter and the corresponding outdoor temperature over an extended period of time is highly recommended. This must be done diligently to obtain an accurate estimate.

2. If the utility's gas bill has a thermal factor (normally in a range of 1.02 to 1.06), multiply the number of meter units consumed in the 24 hour period by this number giving the total Therms used during the 24 hour period, otherwise the meter usage is the total Therms used. A **Therm is 100,000 BTUs**. This total 24 hour Therm usage will include natural gas used for heating but might also include hot water and cooking. I would not reduce the total Therms calculated based

on this unless the hot water or cooking usage is excessive during the period being monitored.

3. By definition, there are 100,000 BTUs per Therm. So, to find the total BTUs used in the 24 hour period, multiply the number of Therms calculated from the meter usage in step 2 by 100,000.

4. The total number of BTUs just calculated is for a 24 hour period. To find the hourly BTUs used, divide the total calculated in step 3 by 24. You now have an estimate of the maximum hourly consumption of BTUs used in your residence. However, there is one more factor that must be introduced in order to find the maximum rate of heat loss per hour, and that is the efficiency of the furnace/boiler that is currently being used. This next step could introduce a significant error into the calculation if the efficiency (%) used is far off from the true value.

5. Multiply the maximum hourly consumption of BTUs calculated in step 4 by the efficiency of the existing heating unit (expressed as decimal, e.g., 80% =.80). Efficiency ratings for gas-fired boilers and furnaces can vary from about 65% to 95% and are designated as **AFUE** (Annual Fuel Utilization Efficiency) and for oil- based heating systems they are called **SEUE** (Seasonal Energy Utilization Efficiency). Heating systems installed prior to about 1992 will most likely have efficiencies in the 50% to 85% range and the ones installed after that in the 80% to 95% range. Estimating on the lower end of these ranges is recommended. Taking the efficiency into account in the load calculation will eliminate the portion of the current heating system's BTU usage that is being lost primarily through the home's chimney. The result is an estimate of the **Maximum Heat Loss per Hour** (in BTUs/hour) that is actually being used to heat the home. In HVAC parlance, this heat loss, or heat load, is usually expressed in Tons. **A Ton of heat load is 12,000 BTUs per hour.**

One assumption made in the above design heat load estimate is that the winter being used to obtain the data for the estimate is an average winter, not an excessively warm one. There is data available from various sources, such as heating degree-days (**HDD**), which will give you an idea whether the data you are using is for an "average" winter. Designers of geo-systems use information known as **bin** data. See *Chapter 11 THE MANUAL-J*.

Another bit of advice for before installing a geothermal heating system is:

> **A homeowner should first spend the money to insulate their home to the maximum extent possible and have an air infiltration blower-door test done before installing a geothermal system. If you omit these steps, your installation cost might be unnecessarily high due to the larger heat pump and loops needed. Any future insulation addition may result in an oversized system which could be troublesome.**

Of course, one has to be diligent in recording the daily natural gas usage in the early stages of planning the implementation of a geothermal heating system in order to perform the above calculation. If the homeowner uses another fuel, whether it is oil, propane, etc., estimating maximum heat loss per hour is much more problematic. I would suggest that if this is the case, a homeowner might try to find a nearby home of the same size, same insulation, that uses natural gas for heating and try to request the information described above from the home's owner. The substitute home should be as similar to the one being sized including the same north/south orientation, the same number of windows in a similar location, insulation levels, etc. A point about gathering heating data should be made here, and that is:

Do not discard your old utility bills as they may be a valuable tool to evaluate the effectiveness (i.e., payback period) of a new geo-system. In fact, constructing a graph that is updated after each bill is received is an easy way to do this.

The following graph that I have constructed is for natural gas usage for a recent 1 year period in a home in northeast USA. A homeowner that currently uses natural gas for heating can establish an accurate measure of heating requirements by recording daily gas meter readings along with daily **HDD** (Heating Degree Days). Local HDD readings can be found in daily newspapers and even on the internet. The HDD per Therm number obtained would be useful when comparing an existing system to a new one. It would even be useful after installing new energy efficient windows or insulation. HDD/Therm could be converted to BTUs/HDD, a fuel independent measure making comparison to a new geo-system straightforward.

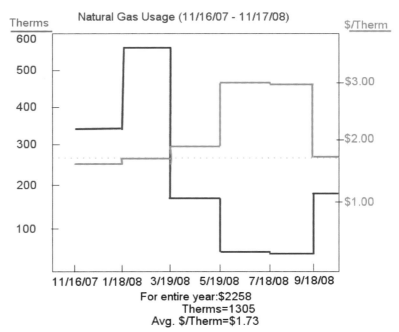

30 The following flowchart summarizes the steps needed to estimate the heating load for an existing residence that uses natural gas as the heating fuel.

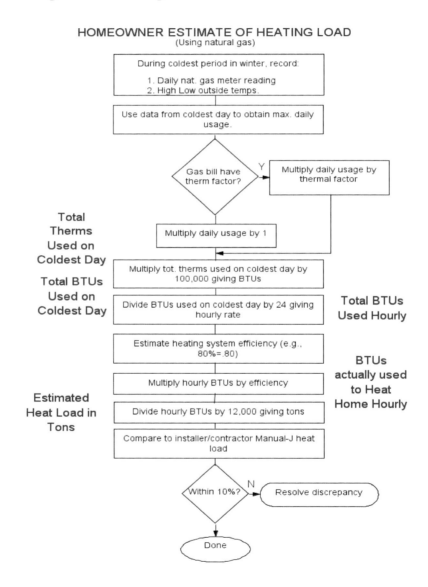

The design Heat Load that was estimated should be compared with an independent **Manual-J** heat load calculation performed by the installers estimating the size of the system. A large discrepancy between the two must be explained.

Heat pumps are rated in **Tons** (usually expressed with a lowercase "t") such as 2 ton or a 3 ton heat pump, etc. The average, well insulated house will more than likely require a 2 to 5-ton geothermal heat pump, depending on the size of the residence.

The reason why a ton of heat is defined as the transfer of 12,000BTU/hr is because it is based on the number of BTUs needed to melt one ton of ice in a 24 hour period.

As an example, the following figures are from an actual natural gas fuel bill for the one month period 12/17/08 to 01/17/09 from a residence in the New York City area.

SAMPLE MONTHLY NATURAL GAS BILL (12/17/08-01/17/09 NYC area)

Number of Days	34
Number of Therms used	402
Cost first 3.4 Therms	$14.87
Cost next 53.3 Therms @$.6114/therm	$32.59
Cost next 345.3 Therms @$.3068/therm	$105.94
Delivery Rate Adjustment @$-0.01271/therm	-$5.11
System Benefit Charge @$.01720/therm	$6.91
MTA Surcharge	$0.28
Total Gas Delivery Charge	$155.48
Gas Supply Charge @$1.18000/therm	$474.36
MTA Surcharge	$.84
4.0000% Sales Tax	$19.01
Supply Sub-total	$494.21
4% Sales Tax on Gas Delivery	$6.22
Bill Charge (incl. Tax & surcharge)	$.82
Total Monthly Bill Charge	$656.73
Effective Cost Per Therm	$656.73/402=**$1.63/therm**

In the above details for the monthly bill, it should be noted that:

MTA Surcharge (Metropolitan Transit Authority) is a mystery to me because it is related to transportation. System Benefit Charge, believe it or not "Recovers the cost of energy efficient programs."

To determine the average cost per therm for the heating season, the total Therms and total $ bill amounts for the period from all of the monthly bills should be used. Using the residence corresponding to the sample natural gas bill (of 1 month) shown on the facing page, the average daily therms used was 402therms/34days= 11.82 therms/day. Let's assume that the highest daily usage during the coldest day was 16 therms, giving an hourly usage of 16/24 = .66 therms/hour. Recalling that one therm is equivalent to 100,000 BTUs, then .66 therms/hour would be 66,000 BTUs/hour. Since this is the total heat usage per hour including wasted heat, that, in effect, goes up the chimney, we must multiply this figure by the heating system's efficiency to get the actual heat load. Assuming a boiler/furnace efficiency of 80%, the actual heating load is .80 x 66,000 BTUs/hour =52,800 BTU/hour. Therefore, the estimate of maximum heating load for this residence would be 52,800/12,000 = 4.4 tons.

The above calculation was made on the basis of real-world measurement using the fuel actually consumed on the coldest day. Some HVAC specialists might argue that this estimate is oversized; that only a few days of the year would this maximum capacity be needed. They would assert that the backup supplemental heat (electric strips are commonly used although natural gas, oil and propane are sometimes used) could provide the heating cushion (also called **heating buffer**) on very cold days. Therefore, the heat pump selected should have a tonnage lower than the actual heating load resulting in a less expensive heat pump/loop installation. While this is a valid point, there are other considerations that must be considered. When the backup electric strips are activated to supplement the geo-system, the additional cost per BTU will be much higher for the electric strips than if the geo-system were able to supply all of the heat. The electric strips operate at 100% efficiency while the geo-system operates at (COP times 100) % efficiency.

Comparison of Heating Cost-----Backup Aux. (Electric) Strip vs Geothermal (Electrical) Heat Pump (for 1,000,000 BTU, average 1 day's usage in very cold weather)

Electricity cost $/Kwh.	Electric Strip (Resistance) $	Heat Pump COP=3 $	Heat Pump COP=4 $	Heat Pump COP=5 $
$0.04	11.72	3.91	2.93	2.34
$0.08	23.44	7.81	5.86	4.69
$0.12	35.16	11.72	8.79	7.03
$0.16	46.88	15.63	11.72	9.38
$0.20	58.60	19.53	14.65	11.72
$0.24	70.32	23.44	17.58	14.06
$0.28	82.04	27.35	20.51	16.41
$0.32	93.76	31.25	23.44	18.75
$0.36	105.48	35.16	26.37	21.10
$0.40	117.20	39.07	29.30	23.44

Table 2.3.1

Note: 1Kwh=3412 BTUs

This cost difference between using backup electric (Auxiliary) heat to supply the buffer heat vs. using the geo-system to supply 100% of heat can be seen in the table above. Of course, there must always be a backup system to provide heat, in heating dominated regions, should there be a failure of the geo-system (i.e., a pump, compressor, etc.) or unusually extreme cold weather. Electric backup heat is recommended because it is simple and reliable but minimum use of the backup system should be a goal.

Another reason not to downsize the tonnage for heating is that the homeowner might decide to add additional living space in the future. Adding a room, utilizing an unheated part of the basement, garage, etc., could be accommodated without major changes to the existing geo-system if the tonnage used to install the system is not downsized from the original Manual-J calculation. It has to be pointed out that the sizing of the system involves not just the size of the heat pump but also the size of the ground loop. Having to add an additional ground loop in the future to increase the system's capacity would be a very expensive proposition and should be avoided. Therefore, **a ground loop that is oversized can be an advantage while a heat pump that is oversized could be a problem**. Today, some geothermal heat pumps are capable of running in multiple stages giving them the ability to adjust to lower heating demands. This reduces the frequent on-off cycling (called **short-cycling**) of an oversized system. Some HVAC personnel recommend installing a heat pump that is 90%-98% of the design heating load and relying on electrical strip heaters to make-up the remainder. I would recommend that the unit be sized for 98%-100% of design heat load. Future increases in electrical cost, which I believe will be substantial, will make the 100% design a prudent one based on the numbers shown in Table 2.2.4. In other words, the system will continue to run at an efficiency of 200+ % rather than the 100% efficiency of electrical heat strips during extremely cold weather.

Another point that some installers make is that by selecting a smaller heat pump and relying more on electric aux. strips, the ground around the loops will have more time to recover from thermal depletion if the strips allow the heat pump and loop to "rest". The claim is that this will allow the system to perform well throughout the winter by not depleting the ground's thermal energy. While this would be true if the ground loop was undersized, it reinforces the recommendation that the ground loops, but not the heat pump, should be somewhat oversized. The more the reliance on heat strips, the higher the monthly electric bill will be.

Insulating Material	R-Value per inch (Min, Max.)
Wood panels	2.5
Vermiculite (loose fill)	2.13-2.4
Perlite (loose fill)	2.7
Rock & slag wool (loose fill)	2.5-3.7
Rock & slag wool (batts)	3.0-3.85
Fibre-glass (loose fill)	2.5-3.7
Fibre-glass (rigid panel)	2.5
Fibre-glass (batts)	3.1-4.3
High-density fibreglass (batts)	3.6-5.0
Cellulose (loose fill)	3.0-3.8
Cellulose (wet spray)	3.0-3.8
Icynene (spray)	3.6
Icynene (loose fill)	4.0
Urea-formaldehyde (foam)	4.0-4.6
Urea-formaldehyde (panels)	5.0-6.0
Polyurethane (rigid panel)	5.5-8.0

Table 2.3.2   R-values of insulation materials

2.4 HEAT LOAD CALCULATION

In order to determine the size of the geothermal heating/cooling equipment needed for a specific residence, in tons, either an actual real-world estimate as previously described for a retro-fit or a heat load calculation must be done. Actually, the heat load calculation should always be done. In HVAC parlance, a **Manual-J** heat load calculation is required. Two terms often used to describe the interior heat content of residences are **Sensible heat and Latent heat**, which are defined as follows:

> **SENSIBLE HEAT** is the heat, or thermal energy, of an enclosed space (or object) that can be transferred from/to that space (or object) via conduction, convection, radiation, or a combination of the three due to a temperature differential between the two spaces but does not involve a change-of-state (i.e., liquid-to-vapor, vapor-to-liquid, etc.) within the space.
>
> **LATENT HEAT**, by comparison, is the heat which is added to/removed from a space (or object) that produces a phase change (i.e. liquid-to-solid, liquid-to-gas, etc.) within the space but does not produce a temperature change.
>
> **SHR** , the Sensible Heat Ratio is the ratio of Sensible heat to the sum of Sensible heat plus Latent heat.

HEAT LOSS-

Loss of residence heat occurs in two main ways:

1. **Radiation/Conduction/Convection**-Heat transmission by way of radiation from the external shell of the residence including the roof, walls, windows and doors, basement walls and

exposed chimney. Also, there is heat transmission by way of conduction/convection with the surrounding air and earth for the same elements. The residential characteristics which influence these losses are:

1. Total exterior surface area of walls and roof and foundation.

2. The total surface area of windows and their R-value (or more commonly, their U-value).

3. Total surface area of exterior doors and their R-value.

4. Whether there is a masonry chimney and how much of it is exposed to the exterior.

5. From the basement- the difference between inside air temperature and, depending on how much the basement is below ground- the external air temperature and surrounding earth temperature.

6. Insulation levels in the walls and roof based on the **R-value** of the insulation. R-value is a measure of resistance to thermal transmission. The higher the R-value, the greater the insulation effectiveness. **U-value** is just the reciprocal of the R-value (i.e., R = 1/U). The table on the facing page displays R-values (per inch of material) for commonly used building insulation materials.

2. Infiltration Heat Losses are divided into two categories:

Sensible Heat Infiltration Loss

Is the heat needed to raise the temperature of infiltrating air to the ambient indoor temperature.

Latent Heat Infiltration Loss

Is the heat content of moisture in the interior air that is lost through exfiltration. The greater the differential between inside and outside humidity levels along with wind intensity, the greater this loss becomes.

BLOCK LOAD CALCULATION

39

A rough estimate of the heating/cooling loads of a residence can be made with what is called a Blockload calculation. When this is done, only the transfer of heat through the building envelope is considered. The internal room layout is not considered. When the Blockload estimate is done, the following characteristics are considered:

1. The north, south, east, west orientation of the residence, which will affect the amount of solar gain.

2. In relation to (1.) above, the amount of window surface area that permits solar gain along with the type of glass used (i.e., single pane, double pane, coatings, etc.).

3. In relation to (1.) above, the presence of building overhangs, trees and shrubbery.

4. The roofing material and the color of the roof tiles.

5. The shape of the roof (i.e. flat, hip, mansard, etc.) including the slope of the roof.

6. The desired interior temperature (i.e., the desired setpoint).

7. The residence location (i.e., the range of outside temperatures in that area).

HVAC specialists take all of these conditions, and many more, into account when they perform a heating load calculation and a cooling load calculation. Less experienced system installers might use a rule-of-thumb to try to estimate strictly based on square footage, 500 to 600 square feet per ton is often used but this estimate is not adequate for installing a finely tuned system.

2.5 THE MANUAL-J LOAD CALCULATION

A more precise heat load calculation than the Blockload should be performed. Since the Blockload calculation ignores the internal structure of the residence, including room layout, duct work, etc., a more accurate load calculation is needed.

 The standard **Manual-J** calculation is normally used in order to size the heating /cooling load. For residential applications, the **ACCA**'s Manual-J (currently eighth edition) is the only procedure recognized by **ANSI** (the American National Standards Institute). It is important from both a cost (installation and ongoing usage) as well as comfort consideration to obtain as accurate a sizing estimate as possible. As of the writing of this book, there are at least five computerized programs that are recognized by the ACCA to perform the Manual-J calculation, they are:

RHVAC   From Elite Software

RIGHT-J   From Wrightsoft

HVAC Wizard From Nitek

HVAC-CALC   From HVAC Computer Systems, LTD.

LOOPLINK   From GeoConnections, Inc.

The sizing of a residential geothermal heating/cooling system can be compared to a window air conditioner. If the air conditioner is too small, it will run continuously and will not be able to maintain the desired temperature (known as the setpoint) and remove the (sensible) heat from the room. By running all the time it will also consume a lot more electricity than it should if it were sized properly. On the other hand, it the window air conditioner is oversized, it will cycle on and off too often. The result is that it will not run long enough to remove the humidity (i.e., the latent heat) in the room resulting in an uncomfortable, "sticky" living space.

Excessive on and off cycles will also cause excessive wear on the motor, shortening the life of the air conditioner.

Unlike the Block Load previously described, which is concerned with the heat transfer through the home's exterior envelope, the Manual-J calculation also takes into account the internal architecture of the home, including room layout, number of stories, the air duct system, etc. *Chapter 11 MANUAL-J* gives an example of a Manual-J report.

2.6 SIZING A RESIDENTIAL GEOTHERMAL SYSTEM (FOR COOLING)

In a cooling dominated region, such as the southern USA, the system is sized based on the **Cooling Load**. As with the Heating Load, there is a specified design condition at which the cooling load is calculated. This is called the **Summer Design Condition**.

Summer Design Condition

The Summer Design Condition, unlike the Winter Design Condition, is affected by three exterior factors instead of just one, they are:

1. The **Summer Design Temperature** is the highest summer temperature which is exceeded only 2 ½% of the time.

2. The average summer humidity or **Summer Moisture Content** as measured in total grains of water per pound of air.

3. The average **range of daily temperatures**, usually assigned one of three values:

    High - cool morning, hot afternoon, cool at night

    Med - warm morning, hot afternoon, warm at night

    Low - hot morning, hot afternoon, hot at night

Cooling Load

Once the Summer Design Condition has been established, the Cooling Load can be calculated for the **Summer Design Interior Temperature**. As with the Heating Load, a computer program is fed all the pertinent information to perform the (Manual-J) Cooling Load calculation. For the geo-system to adequately cool a residence, the cooling load which was calculated must be equal to or greater than the **Heat Gain**, which is described next.

Heat Gain

All sources of heat that can raise the heat content of a residence are evaluated when computing the Heat Gain. The primary sources are:

1. The solar energy that is absorbed by the residence (i.e., solar gain) due to roof color, house orientation, window placement and size, roof shape, etc.

2. Transfer of thermal energy through the exterior envelope of the residence, primarily by conduction and convection from the surrounding air and ground.

3. Thermal energy generated within the residence by appliances.

4. Thermal energy generated within the residence by its occupants.

5. Thermal energy that infiltrates into the residence. Opening a door, cracks within the buildings envelope, exhaust and ventilation systems, clothes dryers, etc., affect the Heat Gain. Both dry warm air and humid warm air (raising the latent heat gain) can enter.

Sizing for cooling dominated regions must be done with even more accuracy than sizing for heating dominated regions. Geo-system units have auxiliary electric heating strips that supplement heating if the unit is not able to extract enough heat from the ground loops to maintain the thermostat's setpoint. In cooling mode, there is no comparable backup or buffer facility to provide additional cooling. Compounding this deficiency, an oversized geo-system in a cooling dominated region could run in a short-cycle mode. The short duration of the on-cycle of the system would result in poor dehumidification.

Estimate of max. daily usage for common non-Geo heating systems in colder climates

System Type	Unit of Measure	BTU/Unit	Efficiency of System	Units Needed to Produce 1,000,000 BTU (About 1 days's requirement)
Nat. Gas	Therm	100,000	65%	15.38 Therms
			75%	13.33
			80%	12.50
			95%	10.53
Oil	Gallon	138,000	65%	11.15 Gal.
			75%	9.06
			80%	8.53
			95%	7.63
Propane	Gallon	90,000	65%	17.09 Gal.
			75%	14.81
			80%	13.89
			95%	11.70
Electricity	Kwh	3412	100%	293 Kwh

Table 2.6.1

Cost Comparison of Geo vs. Conventional heating systems for 1,000,000 BTUs of heat (Approx. 1 day's worth in colder climates).

Energy Type	Formula (cost per 1,000,000 BTU)	Cost (in$) for 1,000,000 BTU
Natural Gas	(cost per Therm x 10)/efficiency	17.8/.80=$22.25
Fuel Oil	(cost per gallon x 7.25)/efficiency	20.30/.80=$25.38
Propane	(cost per gallon x 11.1)/efficiency	32.75/.80=$40.94
Electricity	(cost per kwh x 293)/efficiency	58.60/1.0=$58.60 *
Geothermal COP=2.5	" " /COP	58.60/2.5=$23.44
Geothermal COP=3.5	" " /COP	28.71/2.5=$16.74
Geothermal COP=4.5	" " /COP	28.71/2.5=$13.02
Geothermal COP=5.5	" " /COP	28.71/2.5=$10.65

Table 2.6.2   *Electric heat is 100% efficient

In the table above, the following numbers were used as the price of fuels based on prices in the New York City area which is probably a lot different from what they are today: Natural gas($1.78/Therm), Fuel Oil ($2.80/gal), Propane ($2.95/gal), Electricity($0.020/Kwh). Since geo-system usage costs are totally dependent on local electric costs, potential users should recalculate the above figures using local electric prices. As noted elsewhere, the cost per unit of fuel must include additional charges on the user's bill, including sales taxes and other charges.

2.7 COMPARING GEOTHERMAL HEATING SYSTEMS TO OTHER SYSTEMS

In order to compare geothermal heating systems to other systems, it is necessary to arbitrarily select a quantity of heat (in BTUs) and then compute the amount of each fuel needed to produce the selected quantity of heat. A quantity of heat that is close to the usage of the average house during a cold day, at least in the northeast USA) is about 1,000,000 BTU. Comparisons of different heating systems often use this quantity of heat for comparison purposes. The next step is identify the unit of measure for each type of fuel consumed; a gallon for oil, a therm for natural gas, etc. along with the number of BTUs in each of the units of measure. Specifying a range of efficiency values (e.g. 65%, 75%, 80%, 95%) will then allow us to calculate the number of units (i.e. gallons, therms, etc.) needed to produce the 1,000,000 BTUs for each efficiency specified.

The Table 2.6.1 on the previous page compares the most common fuels used in heating systems and the quantities of their respective units of measure (i.e. gallons, therms, etc.) needed to produce 1,000,000 BTUs based on various system efficiencies. It can be seen that the traditional heating systems cannot have an efficiency greater than 100%. The non-traditional heating systems, including geothermal and air-source heat pumps, have efficiencies greater than 100% and the COP (coefficient of performance) is the analogue of efficiency.

In order to calculate the actual cost (in dollars) to produce the 1,000,000 BTUs, one has to know the price of each of the units of measure (i.e., $/gallon of oil,$/ therm of natural gas, etc.). Table 2.6.2 uses ballpark price values for these different fuels and should be used only as a rough estimate because the real values that apply to you may differ significantly.

Based on the above estimates, which are for a residence located in a northerly location using 1,000,000 BTUs per day during the coldest period of the heating season, a rough comparison of various heating methods can be made. Geothermal heating/cooling system costs, excluding installation costs, are directly related to the local cost of electricity as can be seen from this chart and there might be reduced electric rates available for homes that use a geo-system. It should also be pointed out that natural gas, fuel oil and propane systems consume electricity during their operation and that has not been taken into account in the above table.

It has to be noted that the unit cost for the fuels (i.e., for oil, natural gas, etc.) that are posted by the utility companies are not the actual values that should be used in the above comparisons because the utility companies add-on additional charges to their bill. Various surcharges, sales tax etc., result in an effective unit cost of fuel that can be much higher than the value stated on the energy provider's utility bill.

Whether in a heating dominated region, a cooling dominated region, or a more balanced region, the homeowner must require that a Manual-J heating/cooling load calculation be performed. Preferentially, several installers should be asked to estimate the load (using Manual-J calculation) and their estimates compared.

The actual cost per unit of fuel must be calculated based on the total units consumed and the total dollar cost shown on the fuel bill. All surcharges, taxes, etc., must be included. This is especially important for geo-systems because they use electrical power exclusively. The price per Kilowatt hour (Kwh) advertised by the power utility must be ignored and the actual $/Kwh computed from the utility's monthly bill must be used. Using the numbers for the whole heating season would give a more accurate fuel cost/unit.

Figure 3.1.1

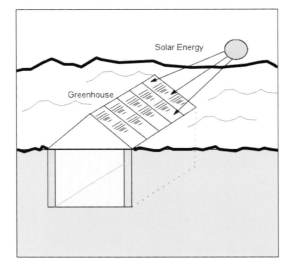

Figure 3.1.2

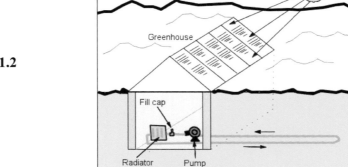

CHAPTER 3 BASIC GROUND LOOP SYSTEMS

3.1 A PRIMITIVE LOOP SYSTEM

Let's start by building a geothermal ground loop system starting with a very basic, or primitive system and then gradually add the features which are used in modern systems. The drawing on the facing page in Figure 3.1.1 is of a below-ground greenhouse structure which was in common use during the 1800s to provide space for growing plants and seedlings during early spring periods when it was still too cold outside for planting.

This structure makes use of both passive solar and passive geothermal energy to provide an internal temperature that is above freezing and conducive to the germination of seeds. The deeper part of the walls and floor area will absorb heat from the surrounding earth which is generally at about 50 degrees F. During the day, when the sun is unobstructed, solar radiation supplements the geothermal absorption raising the internal temperature even further. For its intended purpose, that of providing a cool, above-freezing environment, this setup will work fine. But, if we wanted to use this space for human habitation purposes, we would have to supply additional thermal energy to the space. The traditional way to accomplish this would be to add electric space heaters, a coal or wood stove, or a heating system using oil, natural gas or propane. Compared to these systems, a geothermal closed-loop ground system might be the most cost-effective long term method of providing the additional thermal energy.

Let's modify the structure by purchasing a length of high density polyethylene tubing that is 3/4" wide (inner dimension). This tubing, called **polypipe**, is specially designed for underground use. Right now, we don't know what length of tubing to buy so we arbitrarily buy a 250 ft length. Next, we dig a trench that is 100 feet long , and 6 ½ feet deep starting next to the foundation of the greenhouse. The trench is 3 feet wide. Inside the greenhouse we install a cast iron radiator, similar to the ones commonly used to heat homes with water or steam. We also install an electric water pump to circulate water in the underground loop.

Two holes, about 1 ½" in diameter, are now drilled through the side wall of the green house at the bottom of the trench; both holes at 6 ½ feet deep and three feet apart. One end of the 250 foot polypipe is extended through one of the holes and is connected to the water pumps' inlet. The balance of the poly pipe is extended the length of the 100 foot trench, but before we do that we must do two things:

1. We must remove all stones from the bottom of the trench, and
2. We must add a 6 inch layer of sand to the bottom of the trench and compact it.

These two steps will protect the loop from potential damage from abrasion caused by sharp stones. After laying down the 100 foot length of polypipe, we form a "U" bend of the polypipe at the far end of the trench and lay the balance of the pipe in the trench so that the polypipe is within about 2-3 inches of the sides of the trench. The loose end of the polypipe is now passed through the remaining foundation wall hole and connected to the outlet of the radiator.

Next, we connect the outlet of the water pump with the input of the radiator, inserting a "T" connection, with a capping plug at the top of the "T" as shown in Figure 3.1.2. The capped (fill) pipe allows us to fill the entire system with water. When the cap is in place, we can activate the pump to test the system. If no leaks are found, we then cover the outside loop with 6 inches of sand and use a garden hose to thoroughly soak the sand with water to insure that there are no air pockets between the poly pipe and the sand. Our final step is to refill the trench with the material originally excavated. The material is tamped down after each 6 inch layer is added and then watered down to remove all air pockets. We now have a **Ground Source Heating/Cooling System**. It is a very primitive system, but it will work.

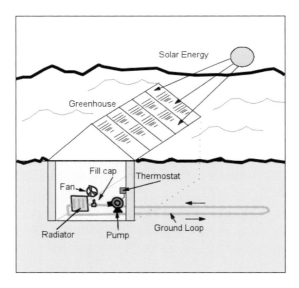

Figure 3.2.1

Our basic system will work, but we will have to manually turn the water pump on and off. Let's remedy this by installing a thermostat that will do this automatically. Let's make our radiator a little more efficient by installing a fan in front of the radiator to move the air through the radiator fins. We wire the fan so that it is turned on when the water pump is activated by the thermostat. Although the polypipe is below ground where temperatures are not expected to fall below freezing, we must add antifreeze. We have to do this for two reasons. First, the polypipe extends into the greenhouse where freezing temperatures might occur. Second, if too much heat is removed from the earth surrounding the polypipe, its temperature could fall below the freezing point of 32 degrees F.

We now have a basic ground source heating and cooling system. We have explained how it would be used for heating purposes but have left out one important consideration about cooling. The thermostat will activate the system when the temperature falls below whatever we set it to. Most modern thermostats have a switch built into them to switch to a cooling operation. Therefore, we must manually change the switch on the thermostat from heating to cooling mode when we want our system to remove heat. The water pump will be activated when the indoor temperature goes above the cooling setpoint value. Whether in heating mode or cooling mode, the system operates the same way. Of course, in cooling mode we would provide a means to block the solar radiation and provide a pan below the radiator to collect condensation.

We installed a polypipe loop that was about 250 feet in length. Since the amount of thermal energy this system can absorb from the ground has to be related to the pipe length, how do we know 250 feet is sufficient? The answer is we don't know. First, the rate of heat loss during the coldest period of greenhouse use must be estimated. This is what is called the heat load of the greenhouse, which is basically the maximum rate of heat loss in BTUs per hour. Then, the diameter of the polypipe, the thermal conductivity of the soil around the pipe, the amount of antifreeze that is added to the water in the pipe and the undisturbed underground temperature, which is different for geographical regions, is used to calculate the loop length. The determination of the proper length of the ground loop will be explored in a subsequent chapter.

We now have a fully functional system as shown in Figure 3.2.1 but there is one major fault with it; it can only provide water for heating our greenhouse at the temperature that is found 6 ½ feet below the ground. If that temperature happens to be 50 degrees F., that is the maximum temperature that our greenhouse can attain, ignoring the solar gain from our windows, when the outside temperature is below 50 degrees F.! What to do? How do we raise the temperature in the greenhouse above the subsurface ground temperature? This question perplexed scientists for a long time before they figured out how to raise the temperature of an object without resorting to some kind of combustion. In the next chapter, we will answer this important question. The geothermal systems described in this book could not work without this discovery. Before we take a detour from improving our primitive geothermal ground loop system to explain the answer to the question just posed, a basic introduction to ground loops used in geo-systems follows.

Figure 3.3.1

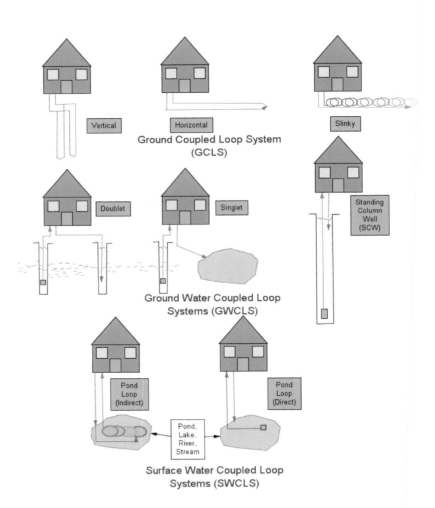

3.3 OVERVIEW OF LOOP SYSTEMS

In the example of the primitive greenhouse geo-system described earlier, a simple, single horizontal loop that circulated water was used. However, there are many different kinds of loop configurations that can be used. Figure 3.3.1 illustrates most of the configurations commonly employed:

Ground Coupled Loop System (GCLS)

1. Horizontal GCLSs consist of one or more loops buried anywhere from 4 to as much as 12 feet below ground. On average, they are usually 5-6 feet below the surface. They are either high density polyethylene (polypipe) tubing that carries water or a water/antifreeze solution or copper tubing that transports a refrigerant in both a liquid and gaseous state. The latter system is known as a Direct Exchange (DX) system.
The layout of horizontal loops can be described as one of two basic configurations:

A. A **simple, Straight loop** that has a U-bend at its center. The two legs of the loop are parallel and often 3 feet apart. Sometimes, multiple loops are placed in the same trench, each overlaying the previous one, separated by a distance of several feet. If there is only one loop in the trench, it is called a two-pipe loop. If a second loop is added, it is a 4-pipe loop system, etc.
B. A **Slinky configuration** is one in which the loops are formed in a flat overlapping pattern. Different degrees of overlap of the loops (called pitch) can be designed. The width (i.e., the diameter) of the loop coils is usually about 3 feet, but they can be wider. Because there is more tubing per linear foot of trench, a shorter trench, compared to the simple, straight loop, can be used with the Slinky configuration. However, longer lengths of the polypipe are required compared to the straight loop for the same installation. The Slinky configuration can only be used with tubing that transports water. It cannot be used with a DX system. A configuration similar to the Slinky is the Spiral configuration, which will be described in *Chapter 6*.

2. Vertical GCLSs require that a borehole or multiple boreholes be drilled to accommodate a simple straight loop. Sometimes 2 loops are inserted in the same borehole. Boreholes are usually about 4 inches in diameter and range in depth from 100 feet to 450 feet for residential systems. Once the loop is inserted in the borehole, a thermally conductive grout is usually used to fill the void between the tubing and the borehole. Vertical GCLSs are often required when there is limited ground surface area which would make a horizontal system impractical. Obviously, there is no Slinky option for Vertical GCLSs.

Ground Water Coupled Loop System (GWCLS)

These systems extract/reject heat from/to subsurface water instead of directly using the ground as a heat sink. They are open-loop systems, meaning they do not circulate the same fixed quantity of water repeatedly through the loop. They continuously obtain "new" water from underground, then extract/reject heat from/to the water and then return it to an underground location. There are 3 basic configurations which are characterized by, among other things, the minimum number of wells required. This minimum number of wells is either one or two:

A. The Singlet, or single well, is the least desirable of the GWCLSs. The well is only used to supply sub-surface water to the heat pump. This is referred to as the **production well**. After the water passes through the heat pump, it is not returned to the aquifer in an **injection well**. The water is directed toward a nearby stream or just dumped on the ground. This method is commonly referred to as a "**pump and dump**" system. Often, a homeowner who has an old water well will, in order to save installation costs, transform the water well to a Singlet geo-system well. Local laws may prohibit the Singlet.

B. The Doublet, or double well, is preferred over the Singlet. Two wells, spaced far apart, are used. Normally a separation of 100 feet is desired. One well is used to withdraw water from the underground aquifer (i.e., the **production well**), passes it through the heat pump to extract/reject heat from/to the water and then delivers the water to the second well (i.e., the **injection well**) for return to the aquifer.

C. The Standing Column Well, or SCW, is a single well that is much deeper and wider than a Singlet. Usually, it is at least 6 inches in diameter and several hundred feet deep. The SCW can only be installed in areas where the subsurface geology consists of porous stone that makes the borehole a rigid cylindrical container that can't collapse. Deep underground water can enter the borehole through the porous stone that surrounds the borehole. The large volume of the well, along with the ability of ground water to enter and recharge the well makes it an effective heat source/heat sink. All of the above open loop systems are sometimes used to provide potable water to the residence in addition to being used for heating/cooling.

Surface Water Coupled Loop System (SWCLS)

These systems use the water from nearby lakes, ponds, rivers and streams. They can be either closed or open loop systems.

Open Loop (Direct) SWCLSs are similar to a horizontal ground coupled loop system (GCLS) except that the water used by the system is not the same water recirculated as in a closed loop system. The benefit of the SWCLS is that the water used, because it is not recirculated, does not vary much in temperature. This makes it more efficient than a GCLS. It also requires a lower water flow rate in the loop, and therefore, less pumping power. The major disadvantage is the impurities and debris that can enter the loop and result in higher maintenance costs of the heat pump. Frequent flushing of the heat pump's heat exchanger coil is required. This configuration is rarely used.

Closed Loop (Indirect) SWCLSs are also similar to horizontal ground coupled loop systems (GCLSs). Unlike the open loop system, they require antifreeze to be mixed with the loop water. The loops are placed at the bottom of a pond or lake. The body of water must be of sufficient depth (usually a minimum of 8 feet) and the surface area of proper size (usually in acres) to accommodate the heating load of the residence. One of the problems encountered with pond loops is the failure to adequately weigh-down the loops. Instances of the loops forming ice around them and floating up and being trapped on the frozen lake surface have been reported.

> **Any open loop system may violate local ordinances. Therefore, the homeowner should inquire about those regulations before considering open loops for their geo-system.**

Direct Exchange (DX) Systems

Unlike water-based systems, **DX** systems use a refrigerant instead of water to extract/reject thermal energy with the ground. Today, most refrigerants are environmentally friendly, unlike freon which was used in the past. Instead of polypipe, copper tubing is used for the loops. Obviously, only closed loop systems apply to DX systems. There are no Slinky configurations and only ground subsurface, not ground water coupled loop systems are used. The basic simple straight loop, used in both horizontal and vertical configurations are the most common for DX systems. Also, a hybrid of vertical and horizontal configurations where the borehole is drilled at an angle into the ground can be used.

In general, DX boreholes and horizontal trench sizes are smaller for DX systems relative to water-based geo-systems because they are able to extract heat more quickly from a given volume of earth. They use the latent heat of vaporization (described in the next chapter) which results in high temperature differentials between the ground and the copper loops.

Icebox

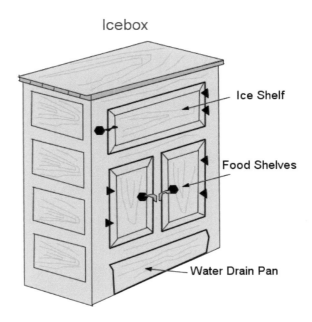

- Ice Shelf
- Food Shelves
- Water Drain Pan

Figure 4.2.1

Comparison of Heat Absorbed-Ice vs. Water
For 1 pound of ice/water at 32 degrees F.

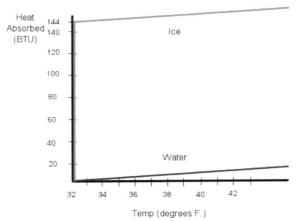

CHAPTER 4 THE REFRIGERATOR

4.1 THE ICEMAN COMETH

There are probably only a few readers of this book who remember the days of the icebox. Long before the advent of the household refrigerator, homeowners and apartment dwellers relied on an icebox to keep their perishable food cold. About 5 feet tall, 3 feet wide and 2 feet deep with an exterior sheathed in wood, often oak, these heavy, cabinet-type structures had a top compartment with hinged doors designed to hold a block of ice. Two mid-level doors sealed the food storage area and a swinging bottom panel hid the drip pan which collected water from the melted ice.

The iceman made his rounds with his horse-drawn wagon and in later years, by truck, carrying blocks of ice 2 feet wide and sometimes at least 6 feet in length. Using an ice pick, he deftly scored the large block of ice to lop off a block that was about 2 feet long. Placing a potato-sack burlap bag on his shoulder, he would use his massive, cast iron tongs to grip the block of ice and holding one handle of the tongs, hoist the block of ice onto his burlap-protected shoulder. He was now able to deliver the ice to the top shelf of an icebox, often after climbing several flights of stairs.

So, how does the ice keep the food within the icebox cold? The answer seems simple: the ice draws heat away from the food, melts and the water flows down to the drip pan. The homeowner had the daily chore of emptying the drain pan. The owners of those iceboxes knew that the water in the drip pan was "ice cold" and that if the ice had completely melted and they put the drip pan filled with this very cold water in the top of the icebox where the block of ice had been, it had almost no cooling effect. The water warmed rapidly and their food would spoil. How could this be? The answer to this question can be deduced from a concept of thermodynamics known as **latent heat of fusion**.

4.2 LATENT HEAT OF FUSION

When a substance, such as a block of ice, undergoes a change of state, also called a **phase change**, to liquid water in the case of ice, its temperature remains constant, at its melting point of 32 degrees F., until all of it has changed to a liquid. During this transformation large amounts of **latent heat** are absorbed from the surroundings. The word "latent' means hidden. This is why the icebox is effective in cooling when it contains a block of ice but not when the block of ice is replaced with the drip pan of "ice cold" water. To show this graphically, we can plot the increase in temperature of a pound of ice and a pound of water at 32 degrees F. if they are both placed in a warm room (say 70 degrees F.). The graph in Figure 4.2.1 illustrates this.

As can be seen in the graph, the magnitude of water's latent heat of fusion (at 32 degrees F.) can be observed. To raise the temperature of one pound of "cold water" by 1 degree F. from 32 degree F. to 33 degrees F. requires 1 BTU of heat energy. Raising the temperature of one pound of ice through the same single degree temperature differential requires the latent heat of fusion of the 1 pound of ice (144 BTU) to melt this ice at 32 degrees F. and another btu to raise the melted water to 33 degrees F. The ratio of heat required for the 1 degree rise in temperature of ice vs. water from 32 to 33 degrees F. is a high 145:1. A similar phenomenon occurs when water undergoes a phase change from liquid to vapor when it is boiled. The heat required to transform the liquid to vapor is called **latent heat of vaporization** and is much higher than the latent heat of fusion (for the same quantity of liquid). Comparing these two quantities of heat for water, we have:

Latent heat of fusion of water = 144 BTU/lb.
Latent heat of vaporization of water =970 BTU/lb.

It is this high heat of vaporization, of a refrigerant instead of water, that makes a modern refrigerator and also a geothermal heat pump an effective instrument in the transfer of heat.

4.3 ENTER…. THE REFRIGERATOR

Modern refrigerators, unlike old iceboxes, do not use water and its latent heat of fusion. Instead, they use refrigerants, which are man-made, fluid compounds as the **working fluid** for heat transfer. The latent heat of vaporization of the refrigerant makes the transfer of large amounts of heat possible. It might sound counterintuitive but these refrigerants transfer heat out of a refrigerator by being boiled. We are conditioned to the incorrect belief that boiling can only take place at relatively high temperatures, such as that of the boiling point of water, 212 degrees F. In fact, all refrigerants, at normal atmospheric pressure (i.e., 1 atm) have a boiling point temperature below that of the temperature of the freezing point of water. There are 3 rules that are necessary to understand the operation of a refrigerator:

> When a refrigerant undergoes a change of state, either from liquid to vapor or vice versa, an extremely large transfer of heat takes place resulting in a change in temperature of some part of the surrounding system. The refrigerant itself remains at the boiling point temperature until all of it has undergone the phase change.
> RULE 1

Just as there is a large quantity of heat absorbed when a liquid is transformed into a vapor (i.e., the latent heat of vaporization), there is an equal amount of heat released when the vapor is transformed back to the liquid state, both of which occur at the boiling point temperature. James Black, a British scientist working on phase-change experiments in 1761, discovered something about vapors that is very important to the subject at hand. At normal atmospheric pressure, water can be vaporized to form steam at 212 degrees F. Likewise, at normal atmospheric pressure, steam can condense to water at this same temperature. Black discovered that if he raised the pressure of the steam, the condensing phase change to water would occur at a higher temperature. We will highlight this second fact that is crucial to understanding the working of a refrigerator and geothermal heat pump:

> When a refrigerant is in the vapor state, increasing its pressure will raise the temperature at which it will condense to a liquid state. In effect, increasing the pressure will raise the liquid refrigerant's boiling point. A household pressure cooker demonstrates this.
> RULE 2

The higher temperature corresponding to the boiling point when the pressure is increased is known as the **saturation temperature**.

The third rule, which I'm sure everyone is well aware of, is the final one needed to understand how a refrigerator works:

The net transfer of heat (i.e., thermal energy) between two objects in close proximity will be from the one at the higher temperature to the object at the lower temperature.

RULE 3

We now have enough knowledge to understand how a modern refrigerator can keep its contents cold. The above three rules are the basis for its operation. The following drawing of the flow of heat in a modern refrigerator demonstrates the three Rules that have just been highlighted.

Refrigerator

The drawing on the facing page is of the back of the refrigerator with the rear wall removed. Beginning at point A, the refrigerant, in liquid form, enters the coiled tubing within the freezer compartment. Because it is under pressure (of about 2-3 atm) its boiling point has been raised (RULE 2) but its temperature (of about 5 degrees F.) is still below its boiling point temperature. Let's assume it has a boiling point (i.e., saturation temperature)of 20 degrees F. at this point. As the liquid refrigerant moves through the freezer coils within the freezer compartment, which is at a temperature higher than that of the refrigerant, heat from within the freezer compartment, and indirectly from the other interior parts of the refrigerator, raises the temperature of the refrigerant to its boiling point of 20 degrees F. (RULE3). This heat absorbing part of the coils in the refrigerator is technically described as the **evaporator**, a necessary component of all geothermal heating/cooling systems.

Most of the liquid refrigerant is vaporized (i.e., boiled), absorbing the large heat of vaporization previously described (RULE 1) and lowering the temperature within the freezer, and by extension, the entire refrigerator interior. The vaporized refrigerant, still at a low pressure (of about 2-3 atm) and temperature of about 20 degrees F. flows toward the **compressor** at C.

The compressor, basically a motorized piston, raises the pressure and temperature of the vaporized refrigerant. The high pressure (of about 8-12 atm), high temperature (let's estimate 120 degrees F.) vapor next passes through the condenser, a section of coiled tubing attached to a metal grill with a large surface area. The high pressure/high temperature vaporized refrigerant in the condenser can now transfer heat to the room in which the refrigerator is located (RULE 3) resulting in a drop in temperature to its boiling point where it undergoes a phase change to liquid. The large latent heat of vaporization (RULE 1) is now passed through the **condenser** grill, which is basically a **radiator** . The heat is then transferred to the room that the refrigerator is in primarily by convection and radiation (RULE 3).

At point D, the vapor has, for the most part, condensed to a liquid but it is still at a relatively high temperature and pressure. In order to return it to its initial condition as it existed at the starting point at A, there is one last component needed. It is a **throttling valve**, called a **capillary tube** and consists of a very narrow length of copper tubing that is usually coiled. The capillary tube implements a throttling function which allows the compressor to build up the necessary pressure in the compressor part of the system. At the output end of the capillary tube, the pressure and temperature of the, mostly liquid, refrigerant is reduced to its initial condition. The cycle can now repeat itself.

We can now continue where we left off in *Chapter 3*. If you recall, our primitive geothermal loop system had reached its limitation, which was that we could only heat the interior of the greenhouse to the maximum temperature of the ground near the ground loop. Since the temperature 6 feet below the ground, on average, is about 50 degrees F., we had to find a way to increase the temperature of the thermal energy that is being delivered to the greenhouse. The operation of the household refrigerator, as described above, provides a solution to that problem. By incorporating the elements of a refrigerator, namely, a refrigerant circuit that includes a compressor, a condenser, a metering (or throttling) valve and a heat evaporator to transfer the heat from underground to the refrigerant in an interior "heat pump" in the primitive loop system of *Chapter 3*, we can achieve a higher temperature in the greenhouse than the maximum loop temperature of 50 degrees F.

The loop itself functions as the evaporator when the system is supplying heat. In cooling mode the ground loop reverses its function and becomes the condenser, rejecting heat to the ground. Geo-systems combine the above 4 elements into a single heating/cooling unit. The units are called **heat pumps**.

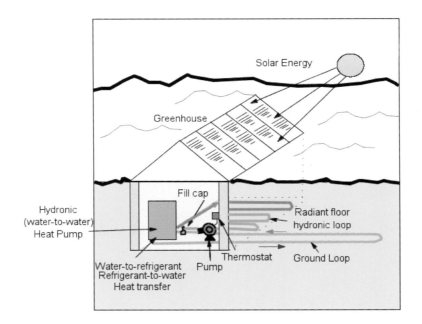

Figure 5.1.1

CHAPTER 5   THE GEOTHERMAL HEAT PUMP

5.1 THE PRIMITIVE LOOP SYSTEM IS ENHANCED

At the end of *Chapter 3*, we had developed a primitive geothermal closed, ground loop system. We reached an impasse in improving the system because, at that point, we had no way of raising the temperature of the water from the loop that had extracted heat from the ground. The previous chapter, *Chapter 4*, explained how, using the basic principle that applies to a common household refrigerator, the temperature of a fluid can be raised to a higher temperature without using some form of combustion.

The basic scientific principle that applies to the transfer of heat in a refrigerator, known as the Carnot Cycle, requires several elements to operate. A compressor, an evaporator, a condenser and an expansion valve are needed. These elements permit a refrigerator to operate and they are the same elements that a heat pump requires. Returning to the primitive system of *Chapter 3*, we have added a basic heat pump as shown in Figure 5.1.1. This heat pump supplies warm water to radiant heat tubing embedded in the concrete floor of the greenhouse.

Let's summarize the operation of the system. When the thermostat calls for heat, the pump that circulates water in the ground loop kicks in and draws the water (which is near the temperature of the ground surrounding the loop) into the heat pump unit. The heat exchanger coil of the heat pump, which contains a liquid refrigerant (normally R410A or R22), absorbs heat from the ground loop water (which is generally at a temperature in a range of 30 degrees to 55 degrees Fahrenheit). The refrigerant is vaporized and then compressed to raise its temperature and pressure and transfers this heat to the condenser coil of the heat pump (at a temperature of 100 to 120 degrees Fahrenheit). The interior heat distribution system of the greenhouse, in this instance water-based (hydronic a/k/a **water-to-water**), absorbs heat from the high temperature condenser coil of the heat pump. Our primitive loop system could just as well have been a **water-to-air** system. The thermostatic activation of the ground loop water pump also activates the second water pump in our system which circulates water within the interior radiant heat system.

There are two elements which must be added to the system to make it functional. Since the water in the ground loop might be subject to below-freezing temperatures, **anti-freeze** must be added. An environmentally friendly anti-freeze, ethylene glycol is often used. Since our geothermal system must be able to cool as well as heat, there must be a way to reverse the system's operation. By adding a **reversing valve** within the heat pump, the direction of flow of the refrigerant can be reversed thereby reversing the roles of the evaporator and condenser.

A special thermostat is used which allows the reversing valve to be activated manually with a switch on the thermostat or automatically based on the temperature settings (i.e., heating and cooling **setpoints**) of the thermostat for heating and cooling.

The refrigerant used in almost all geothermal heat pumps is known as R-410A, a much more environmentally safe refrigerant than the older R-22 refrigerant. R-22 refrigerant cannot be used in new air conditioners and heat pumps after 2010. Its price is expected to increase after that based on a limited supply. Therefore, make sure that a new heat pump uses **R-410A** refrigerant.

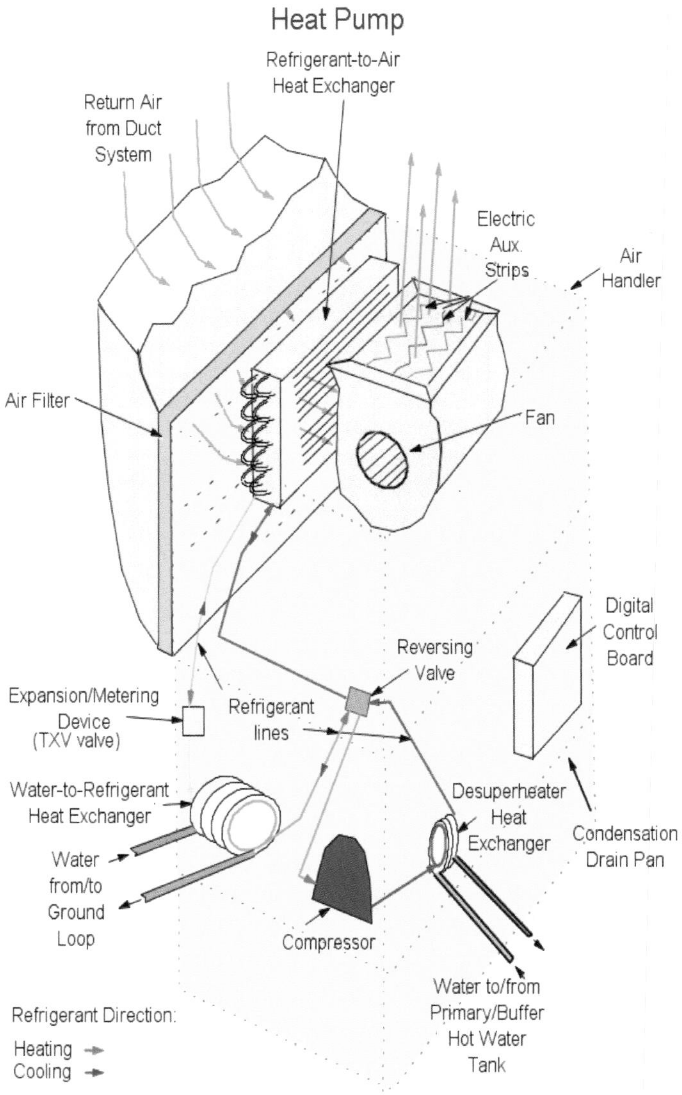

Figure 5.2.1

Heat Pump

Refrigerant-to-Air Heat Exchanger

Return Air from Duct System

Electric Aux. Strips

Air Handler

Air Filter

Fan

Digital Control Board

Reversing Valve

Expansion/Metering Device (TXV valve)

Refrigerant lines

Water-to-Refrigerant Heat Exchanger

Desuperheater Heat Exchanger

Condensation Drain Pan

Water from/to Ground Loop

Compressor

Water to/from Primary/Buffer Hot Water Tank

Refrigerant Direction:

Heating →
Cooling →

Unlike our primitive loop system, water-to-air geo-systems, which are much more common today compared to a water-to-water system, require an air duct system. An **air handler**, which is usually integrated into the water-to-air heat pump unit, contains a fan which moves air rapidly over the heat pump's condenser coil into the duct system. The major advantage of a water-to-air geo-system is that air conditioning is easily supplied using the ductwork. Another advantage of the water-to-air system is that a humidifier can be installed in the duct system along with an auxiliary resistance heating strip which supplements as well as serves as a backup heat source. However, a possible additional expense associated with a water-to-air system is:

> **A Water-to-Air geothermal system often requires that the duct work within an existing home be replaced with a larger one. The reason is that the air temp. in a geo-system is much lower than in a conventional system and the quantity of air that must be circulated to perform the same heat transfer is much greater. This can add a considerable expense to the cost of the system.**

If the air duct system is undersized for the geo-system, the air must be pumped at a higher rate which often results in uncomfortable drafts and noise complaints as well as a lower efficiency. Even though our primitive geo-system is a water-to-water system, the use of such systems is limited today because:

> **Hot water space heating requires water circulating within the radiators (or convectors) to be at a fairly high temperature (of about 160 degrees F.) whereas heat pumps are limited to about 120 degrees F., severely limiting the use of water-to-water heat pumps. However, in radiant heating systems, especially where a large thermal mass is used, they are viable because much lower temperature water is sufficient to provide heat. Radiant systems require water temperatures in the range of 85-140 degrees F.**

HYDRONIC (Water-to-Water) SYSTEMS

The comments above explain why most residential geo-systems are water-to-air rather than water-to-water systems. However, there are many radiant heating systems that use hydronic (i.e., water-to-water) heat pumps. Some of these systems use a buffer tank between the heat pump and the sub-floor radiant tubing, others omit the buffer tank and feed the radiant tubing directly. There are even a few hybrid systems that combine the water-to-air and water-to-water functions within the same heat pump. These systems allow air conditioning capability, which would not be possible with just a water-to-water system. **WaterFurnace's Synergy 3** heat pump is an example. Radiant heating systems, especially those with large thermal mass components, such as concrete slabs, can be far superior, on a cost-of-use basis, to air duct systems. This would occur if time-of-day electric billing is available. The system could be set up to run the heat pump, extracting heat from the ground, during the daily low rate period (i.e., at night) to heat a water storage buffer tank. During the daytime, the heat pump would be inactive allowing the ground loops to "rest." All calls for heat would only activate the pumping of water from the storage tank through the radiant tubing circuit.

Heating systems that circulate air in ducts are more problematic than radiant systems in terms of air quality. Mold, bacteria and dust can accrete within the duct system, necessitating periodic cleaning of the ducts and filter. Forced air circulation systems alter the "envelope delta P" (i.e., air pressure differential) of the structure. During the heating season this pressure differential forces warm air out through cracks, open doors, etc. This **exfiltration** lowers the efficiency of the heating system. Likewise, during the cooling season, the pressure gradient could cause the **infiltration** of humid outdoor air. These undesirable conditions don't occur with a radiant system. Obviously, the installation cost of a radiant system is higher.

DUCTLESS MINI-SPLIT SYSTEMS

Most heat pumps are **all-in-one** (also called **packaged**) **units** as shown in Figure 5.2.1. The air handler, heat exchanger, etc., are all enclosed in a single, refrigerator-size steel cabinet. These units are used when there is a central ductwork distribution system available.

There is an alternative for existing homes that do not have an air duct system. This is called a ductless mini-split system. Air handlers, which contain refrigerant-to-air heat exchangers and fan units, are built into separate units and installed at various points in the residence. The base unit, which is usually installed in the basement, supplies refrigerant to each air handler unit. The refrigerant lines, with electric control wires, can pass through a 3 inch opening. Each unit has its own thermostat, effectively creating a zoned system. This type of system can attain efficiencies higher than the packaged unit because as much as 30% of heat loss can occur in duct systems. Leaks in duct systems and passage of the ducts through unheated areas can dissipate a lot of the heat intended for conditioned spaces.

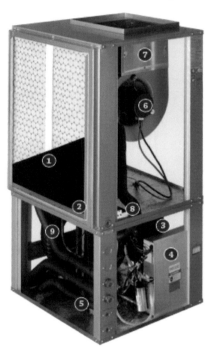

Figure 5.9.9 All-in-One Heat Pump
Courtesy Hydron Module

1. Coated Air Coils
2. Stainless Steel Drain Pan
3. Copeland 2-stage Scroll Compressor
4. Digital Controls
5. Optional Desuperheater
6. ECM Air Blower Motor
7. Optional Aux. Heater
8. Condensate Overflow Sensor
9. Cupro-Nickel Coaxial Heat Exchanger

In *Chapter 3*, there was an explanation of how a geo-system should be sized. It is important to obtain as accurate an estimate of the design heating load as possible in order to install the proper size heat pump. An oversized unit will result in an unnecessary high installation expense. Some would say that this would also result in a system that would turn on and off too frequently (known as **short-cycling**) and therefore shorten the life of the heat pump. To a certain extent this might be true but the better heat pumps have multi-stage compressors and variable speed air fans (in water-to-air systems) that mitigate this concern.

When evaluating the heat pump to be used, the following guidelines should be used:

BASIC HEAT PUMP SELECTION CRITERIA

1. Select the **proper size** (in tons) of the heat pump based on the Manual-J heat load calculation. Size increments of ½ ton are common. See section *Chapter 11 Manual-J* on sizing of geo-systems.

2. A **Dual-stage compressor** is more efficient because it operates at a lower (first stage) energy level when weather is milder, thereby eliminating "short-cycling." Running for a longer period of time allows a dehumidifier to remove household moisture more effectively and allows more hot water (using a desuperheater) to be produced. The heat pump is sometimes labeled as 3 stage if a backup electrical resistance strip (the third stage) is included with the 2 stage compressor. This description can be confusing.

3. A **Scroll-type compressor** is preferred over piston type compressors because it is quieter, has a longer life and uses less electricity.

4. For water-to-air systems, the fan blower motor should be an **ECM** (Electronically Commutated Motor) which varies air speed based on compressor stage and produces a more comfortable flow of air from the registers.

5. Either a packaged system (where all components are contained in one unit) where there is a central duct system or a split system (where the air handler is in a remote location relative to the compressor) can be selected.

6. A **Desuperheater** (a coil to heat domestic hot water using the geo-system) is an optional feature of heat pumps. It is recommended that they be purchased with the heat pump and, as will be described later, an additional buffer hot water tank. Tax incentives for geothermal systems may not apply if the desuperheater is not included. (See section 5.4 for info on desuperheaters).

7. **Drain Pan,** which collects condensation, should be made of stainless steel.

8. **Multi-stage thermostat** should be used. There is mixed opinion on whether a setback option should be used on geothermal system thermostats, but the t-stat should have this function.

9. Heat Pump unit should be **Energy Star rated** (COP is 3.3 or higher, EER is 14.1 or higher, for a closed loop system).

10. The **refrigerant** used in the heat pump should be the ozone friendly R-410A and not R-22, which is being phased out after 2010.

11. For open loop systems, the water-to-refrigerant **heat exchange unit** should be made of cupronickel (an alloy of copper and nickel).

12. Flexible, canvas-type boot connection between the ductwork and heat pump to dampen sound vibrations as well as a pad below the heat pump should be installed.

13. The **warranty** of the heat pump should be at least 10 years and installer should be bonded, insured and licensed in your state.

The tax incentives for installing a geothermal system, which as of this moment is a 30% Federal tax credit. Currently, most of the heat pump manufacturers listed in *Appendix C* have EnergyStar rated equipment. There are websites that can provide more up-to-date information including the specific heat pump models that are EnergyStar compliant, such as:

http://energybible.com/geothermal_energy/energy%20star%20heat%20pumps.html

In addition to the above items on the check-list for heat pumps, it is recommended that a whole-house electrical surge protection system be installed. There are a lot of expensive electronic components in the heat pump and it makes good sense to protect these assets.

What is the electrical cost to run a heat pump?

A rule of thumb for the electrical requirement, excluding aux. heat, is that each ton of heat pump capacity will need to use one Kilowatt of power. Therefore, depending on how many hours during the day the heat pump is active, the daily cost can be estimated to be:

Daily Electrical Cost of Heat Pump =
tonnage of heat pump X 1 KW/ton X hours used in a day X cost per KWH

There are concerns about which expenditures will be eligible for the 30% Federal Income Tax credit. My advice would be not to do a piecemeal installation of the geo-system. Have all the work done by the system installer and have him provide an invoice itemizing all of the components, including:

1. Cost of the Loop installation including excavation, purging loops, adding antifreeze, etc.

2. Cost of Heat Pump installation including backup heat strips.

3. Cost of the Desuperheater (if not supplied with the heat pump).

4. Water-to-air system ductwork or water-to-water system radiant installation. New ductwork

could be expensive if the existing duct system is too small.

5. Upgrade to electrical service if required.

6. All system monitoring devices that measure loop temperature, pressure, etc.

7. All other expenses, itemize.

If you have to upgrade your electrical service from 100 amps to 200 amps, for example to accommodate the installation of the system, don't do this long before the installation of the system. To repeat, have everything necessary to run the system done at the same time to avoid any problem with taking the full 30% tax credit (in the USA).

5.3 HEAT PUMP INSTALLATION

One of the most basic items required for the installation of a heat pump is an adequate opening (i.e., doorway) to bring the unit into the home. Sometimes this is not considered before the unit arrives, causing last minute alterations to the entranceway. Heat pumps can usually be installed in either a vertical orientation, which is most common, or horizontal orientation when space constraints exist. They should be positioned so that there is adequate room around them to facilitate electrical and plumbing connections. The ability to insert and remove an air filter should be considered. Left or right air return (from duct) option must be specified.

The heat pump and its auxiliary equipment including piping and hot water tank should not be installed in an area where the ambient temperature falls below 50 degrees F. If it is, the efficiency (i.e., its COP) will be lower than expected because it will deliver excessive heat to its cool location at the expense of heat delivery to the living quarters. The heat pump equipment should never be exposed to below freezing temperatures to avoid severe damage. The warranty of the heat pump can be voided if is exposed to temperatures that are too low. The heat pump unit should rest on a vibration absorption pad that is larger than the base of the unit. A flexible connector, often made of canvas, that connects the metal ducts to the unit should be installed for sound and vibration reduction.

When a fossil fuel heating system is replaced with a geothermal heating system, there is one consideration that might be overlooked. The system being replaced most likely supplied the basement with a lot of heat, eliminating the possibility of frozen water pipes. A geo-system does not match this level of heat supplied to the basement. Therefore, the homeowner should provide for some kind of low level alternate heat supply in the basement or additional insulation to insure that pipe freezing will not occur.

Once the unit is fully assembled, both electrically and plumbing-wise, the ground loop must be purged of air and dirt. HVAC personnel connect what is known as a **flush cart**. This consists of a powerful water pump of at least 1.5 horsepower that is used to perform a forward-and- backward flush of the ground loops.

After purging the ground loops of air, antifreeze is added. The amount of antifreeeze added is very important for freeze protection. An excessive amount will make the loops less efficient at transferring heat from the ground. Depending on the season in which the loops are pressurized, the specified water pressure is applied. For summer, 40-50 psi, and for winter, 50-75 psi of pressure is used. The antifreeze used is specially designed for use in ground loops. The homeowner should make sure that pressure/temperature ports are installed so that the water temperature and pressure measurements on the loop side of the heat exchanger can be monitored. These ports are often referred to as "**pete's ports**." The pressure drop across the heat exchanger should be about 5 psi for a closed loop water-based system. The control board that is inside the heat pump cabinet has several dip switches. It is recommended that the homeowner take a photo of this board after installation so that a permanent record of the initial settings can be referenced should any subsequent changes be made.

Figure 5.4.1

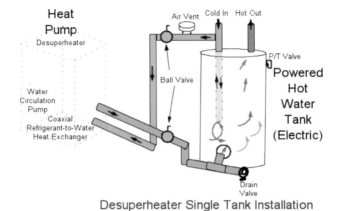

Desuperheater Single Tank Installation

Figure 5.4.2

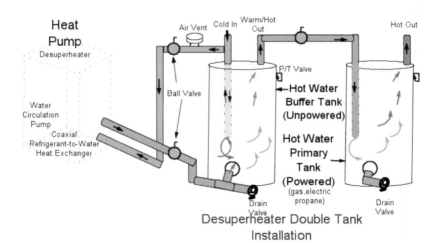

Desuperheater Double Tank Installation

The **Desuperheater**, also known as a **Hot Water Generator (HWG)**, is considered an **optional** component of a heat pump by the some of the heat pump manufacturers. Its purpose is to extract excess heat from the heat pump to warm water used in the household (i.e., for domestic hot water usage). In effect, it uses the first (hottest) section of the refrigerant tubing that extends from the compressor forming a small heat exchange coil that is used to provide heat for the water. This is often referred to as "**superheat**." In the summer when the system is in cooling mode, if there were no desuperheater coil, the heat transferred from the interior air to the main heat exchange coil would normally be dissipated in the ground loop. Therefore, it is during the summer that the desuperheater is most efficient, often being able to provide 100% of domestic hot water needs. In the winter, the heat from this coil (of about 10% of total) is "stolen" from the heat that would be used to warm the home. During spring and fall periods (sometimes referred to as the "**shoulder seasons**") when neither heating nor cooling is needed and the geo-system is inactive, the desuperheater supplies 0% of the domestic hot water. **The desuperheater is a supplementary source of domestic hot water**. When the geo-system is in heating mode, at least 30% of the hot water demand is supplied by the desuperheater. The desuperheater is productive only when the heat pump (i.e., the compressor) is running. Whether in heating or cooling mode, the most hot water is produced when the heat pump runs for a long continuous period. Therefore, in both extreme hot or extreme cold regions, the desuperheater can supply almost all of the domestic hot water needs.

During extremely cold periods, the desuperheater, because it "steals" 10% of the heat that would normally be used to heat the house, is often shut off during these periods in order to boost the heat to the residence. Depending on the heat pump used, this may require, for example, the removal of a fuse. However, there are some heat pumps that automatically disable the desuperheater when the heat pump runs in second stage when in heating mode. The "heat stealing" effect of the desuperheater is a reason to make sure the heat pump selected and loop field installed are not undersized, especially in heating dominated regions.

Based on the seasonal variation in the hot water output of desuperheater, it is obvious that an independent, primary hot water heater is required. Primary hot water heaters, that are electric, are commonly used with a geo-system/desuperheater configuration for several reasons. First, they will outlast almost all other types of "flame-based" hot water heaters. Second, since it does not require a chimney or flue pipe, it can be located almost anywhere, preferably close to the heat pump. Third, some electric hot water heaters have a lifetime warranty (for the initial purchaser). And finally, electric water heaters have a slower recovery rate, the time it takes to reheat water in the tank. This means that with a single electric hot water tank, the desuperheater can "compete" with the electric water heater to heat the water in the tank. Water passing through the desuperheater unit has its temperature increased by about 5-10 degrees F. (i.e., the **desuperheater delta "T"**). Depending on how long the heat pump is run, which is the same length of time the desuperheater runs, water in the single hot water tank can quickly reach its high temperature setpoint, normally 120 degrees F. to 140 degrees F.

It might seem superfluous but it is recommended that two hot water tanks be installed in a geo-system with a desuperheater; here is the rationale. If only a single hot water tank is used, it will be set to maintain the normal temperature required in the household (say 130 degrees F.) At any given time, the geo-system may or may not be running and therefore, the desuperheater may be adding heat to the hot water tank or may not be. Since the desuperheater cannot add more heat to the tank when the tank it is already at setpoint temperature (of 130 degrees in the tank in this example), its capacity to deliver the excess or wasted heat of the geo-system is compromised. To get around this problem a second, unpowered hot water tank is added between the primary tank and desuperheater.

The second hot water tank is called a **buffer tank** or **preheat tank** and is directly connected to the desuperheater. It is not hooked up to electricity or any other fuel source and merely acts as a storage tank (i.e., it is unplugged). The desuperheater can now heat the water in the buffer tank independent of the condition of the primary tank. The buffer tank's output, with warm or hot water, feeds the input to the primary tank so that the primary tank does not have to raise the temperature of incoming, normally cold, water to 130-140 degrees F., thereby lowering its fuel usage cost, regardless of the type of fuel used. With a buffer tank, the primary hot water tank does not have to be electric. If the buffer tank were able to be kept at a temperature near 120 degrees F., for example, the primary tank would only have to raise its incoming water by 10-20 degrees F., in this example. As noted, electrical hot water tanks have a greater longevity than other types, but they are more expensive. It is recommended that the buffer tank be at least an 80 gallon tank to take full advantage of the desuperheater. Expect to pay $800 to $1000 for the best 80 gallon electric hot water tanks (with a lifetime guarantee). By using a buffer tank, the primary tank can be selected from just about any type of water heater, including the on-demand, natural gas tankless type. If the quality of the water supplied to the residence from the city, town or well is of very poor quality with dissolved minerals, some heat pump manufacturers recommend that a desuperheater not be used because of the necessity of frequent cleaning maintenance. However, not installing a desuperheater, at least as of the date this is written, may exclude the current 30% Federal tax credit.

There are a few ways the domestic hot water tanks (the primary and buffer) can be connected to the desuperheater:

Figure 5.4.1 illustrates the single, electric tank setup with desuperheater.

Figure 5.4.2 illustrates the double, buffer tank setup with desuperheater.

GUIDELINE FOR DESUPERHEATERS

1. The desuperheater has a high temperature cutout switch on the return line from the hot water tank usually set at 125-140 degrees F. This switch senses excessively high temperature and must not be removed, for safety reasons. The cutout switch can be moved, by a qualified HVAC person, to the water line leaving the desuperheater if the water tank temperature is too hot.

2. The desuperheater pump must not be run without water in the desuperheater-tank circuit. Damage to the pump would result without water flow.

3. During installation, all of the air must be purged from the desuperheater-hot water tank circuit. An air vent is recommended in the water inlet to the desuperheater. It should be located at the highest point.

4. The water pipes to and from the desuperheater must be copper ($\frac{1}{2}$ or $\frac{5}{8}$ inch) and insulated.

5. The desuperheater delta "T" (the difference between the entering and leaving water temperature of the desuperheater) should be 5 to 12 degrees F.

6. Maintenance of desuperheaters includes periodic flushing and cleaning of the desuperheater water circuit including the hot water tank connected to the desuperheater.

7. Shutoff ball-type valves should be installed in both the in and out legs of the desuperheater water lines to facilitate replacement/repair, including flushing, of the hot water tanks and for possible adjustment of the desuperheater water circuit delta "T".

When the buffer tank is used, the primary hot water tank that is fed by the buffer tank can also be an "on-demand" **tankless hot water heater**. As the name implies, no hot water is stored; it is fired up when a faucet is opened to trigger the unit's heater. However, a tankless hot water heater that will work with entering water that is warm or hot must be selected. Electric tankless water heaters are not recommended due to both the high installation and usage expense.

One of the problems with tankless hot water heaters is the **"cold water sandwich"** effect. If the water flow rate falls below a certain level, when a faucet is only slightly open or when it is quickly closed and opened, cold water quickly replaces the hot water that was flowing for a brief period. In non-geo systems, the "cold water sandwich" effect is especially noticeable when the tankless unit is drawing water directly from the cold water supplied to the residence. With a buffer tank, this effect is mitigated because it contains warm or hot water. However, there is one potential problem with the tankless hot water heater/buffer tank setup. If the homeowner goes away on vacation and the warm water in the buffer tank remains stagnant for a period of time, bacteria could develop within the buffer tank. If nothing were done to remedy this condition, when the hot water was eventually used, the "cold water sandwich" effect could deliver the tainted water when the hot water flow rate was abruptly varied as previously described. There are two possible ways to correct this situation. The first way is to purge all of the water in the buffer tank after a long period of non-use (e.g., after a vacation). The second way is to energize the buffer tank after returning from vacation and raising its temperature to 140 degrees F. temporarily to destroy any bacteria in the tank.

This undesirable situation could also occur with a regular, non-tankless, hot water primary tank, especially an electric one. If a high volume demand exhausts the primary tank, water is drawn into it from the buffer tank. The electric hot water tank may not be able to quickly raise the temperature of the entering water to a high enough temperature to kill all bacteria before it is passed into the hot water supply lines. Therefore, if the water in the buffer tank remains stagnant for an extended period of time, regardless of the type of primary tank, the water in it should be drained or the buffer tank's heating mechanism temporarily activated to raise the tank to a high temperature.

There is no general rule about the relative sizes of the primary and buffer tanks. The water-use needs of the residents will have a major impact on the sizing of the tanks. If the primary hot water tank is electric, it is reasonable to install a larger buffer tank (such as an 80 gallon). One reason for this is the heat pump, using its desuperheater, will heat the water at a COP greater than 3, compared to the primary electric hot water heater at a COP not greater than 1, thereby increasing the efficiency and lowering the electric cost. Depending on the relative cost of natural gas vs. electric, this might not be true of a natural gas primary water heater. Also, the larger buffer tank will have water at a lower temperature than a smaller buffer tank, permitting a higher rate of transfer of heat from the desuperheater. The result is the larger buffer tank will have a lower temperature than a smaller buffer tank but higher thermal energy content. If an existing hot water tank is going to be used when the geo-system is installed, it should be thoroughly drained and cleaned of any sediment, especially if used as a buffer tank.

5.5 AUXILIARY HEAT

The Auxiliary heat strips (**Aux units**) are optional, backup heating elements that are installed within the air handler unit. Their purpose is to provide emergency backup heat if the geo-unit fails, which is rare, or to supplement the heat pump if outside temperature drops to low levels and the geo-unit cannot supply sufficient heat based on the thermostat setting. The outdoor temperature at which the heat pump could not maintain setpoint is called the **Balance Point** (temperature). This is not a precise number because various factors such as wind conditions, solar gain and thermostat setting affect this temperature. The auxiliary unit consists of resistance strips which are electrical resistance coils similar to that in a household toaster. Although they are considered optional, they should be installed in every water-to-air heat pump except in very warm southern regions that rarely require heating. If the compressor should fail, there will at least be some source of heat, even though it would be very expensive. And, if the homeowner is away, the backup heat will automatically activate. I would also recommend some form of supplementary backup heat that does not rely on electrical power, such as a wood stove or natural gas fireplace.

Some geothermal HVAC specialists advocate reducing the size of the heat pump (in tons) and relying on the aux unit, or other fuel based units that can tie into the ductwork to make up the difference during the brief extremely cold periods. Their logic is that the heat pump would be oversized if it could handle the coldest conditions (less than a dozen days, they say, of the year) without resorting to aux heat and therefore, the installation of the full heat-load based unit would inflate the necessary installation cost. I do not agree with this view. Especially in parts of the USA where electrical costs are high (such as the northeast) and where the future price of electricity is totally unpredictable, I believe it would be prudent not to undersize the heat pump in the hope that the aux unit would have minimal electric-cost impact, long-term. As mentioned previously, if a homeowner decides to add additional living space: an addition, converting an unheated basement, etc., the heat pump (and ground loops) may not have to be upgraded if the system is sized for full load conditions.

Sometimes the aux unit will kick in even though the outside temperature is not especially cold, resulting in unnecessarily high electric bills. This is more likely to occur if the homeowner sets the thermostat lower at night and raises it the next morning and the heat pump strains to recover. In order to reduce this negative effect, an outdoor cutout thermostat can be installed (for around $150). The aux heat will not be activated if the outside temperature does not fall below the setpoint of the outside thermostat. If the homeowner is going to be away from the house for an extended period of time, the outside lockout thermostat should be disabled for that period.

Aux heating strips are usually installed in heating capacities from 5 Kw to 20 Kw, often with the ability of the heat pump to incrementally add each of the 5 Kw strips as needed. Based on the conversion of Kw to BTU/hr:

1 ton (heating) = 12,000 BTU/hr= 3.51 Kw

The heat strips have the following heating capacity in tons:

5 Kw = 5/3.51 X 12,000 = 17,040 BTU/hr = **1.42 tons**
10 Kw = 10/3.51 X 12,000 = 34,200 BTU/hr = **2.85 tons**
15 Kw = 15/3.51 X 12,000 = 51,240 BTU/hr = **4.27 tons**
20 Kw = 20/3.51 X 12,000 = 68,400 BTU/hr = **5.70 tons**

From the above data it can be seen that a 20 Kw heat strip can supply a heat load of 5.7 tons. Therefore, it doesn't make sense, from a cost perspective, to install 20Kw of heat strip capacity on a system that has a design heat load of 4 tons or less. Also, the heat strips are usually electrically wired to their own, exclusive circuit (and circuit breaker). Installing oversized heat strip capacity would also require a more expensive electrical (i.e., larger wire size) circuit installation. The circuit breaker should not be turned off to disable aux heat from being activated. Not only will that prevent emergency backup heat from being engaged, it would mask a potential system malfunction from being detected as described below.

Some installations use an outdoor lockout thermometer to prevent auxiliary heat strips from being activated when the weather is above a preset temperature. While this may be a reasonable way to offset expensive use of the backup strips when the thermostat has been set back during the night and the heat pump has to "catch up" the next morning, there is a downside to this practice. The backup heat strips are the "canary in the coal mine" in my opinion. When outdoor temperatures are not too cold the backup strips should not be automatically activated, assuming no setback. If they are, then this is an early warning indication that something is wrong. It is better to be alerted to the problem in October or November, rather than in the frigid weather of January. My advice would be not to use thermostat setbacks nor outdoor aux strip lockout thermostats.

Geo-systems require a more advanced thermostat, a digital one, rather than the one used on conventional heating systems. The setting of a temperature, called a **setpoint**, is required for both the desired heating and cooling temperatures. A minimum temperature separation (in degrees Fahrenheit) between the heating and cooling setpoint must be maintained.

The difference between these two setpoints is known as the "**dead band**" and is generally at least 2 degrees F. This prevents unnecessary cycling between heating and cooling modes when the AUTO operation mode is selected.

All geo-system thermostats have these basic functions:

HEAT (on)
COOL (on)
AUTO (can automatically switch between heating and cooling mode...dead band, as mentioned, should be at least 2 degrees F.) There is a built-in time delay for the changeover. For example, if the system is working in the cooling mode and the heating setpoint is raised substantially, it might take up to 30 minutes for the system to change from cooling to heating mode.
EMER (when selected, emergency mode disables the compressor and uses auxiliary backup heat (either electrical resistance strips or other types).
OFF   (deactivates entire system)
CURRENT TEMPERATURE is displayed
SETPOINT TEMPERATURE (is displayed for active mode)

Some thermostats display a special symbol for the system mode:
Flame symbol - For heat mode; might have a flashing flame symbol when system is using electrical auxiliary heat in emergency mode or the geo-system cannot satisfy heating requirement by itself.
Snowflake symbol - Cooling mode.

Some thermostats have a **BATT** (battery) indicator which lights up when the battery needs to be replaced.

FAN control, if present, will have an auto(matic) or continuous option. With continuous option, the fan does not shut off when the geo-system is not active. This will increase electrical usage based on the type of motor in the air handler. An **ECM** blower motor will use significantly less electricity than a **PSC** blower. The continuous option is used to help distribute warm or cool air evenly throughout the home and requires that the air filter be checked more frequently. One of the negative consequences of using the continuous fan option is that in high humidity environments, the moisture that condenses on the air handler heat exchanger coils may be re-circulated into the duct system because it does not have a chance to drain into the pan at the bottom of the air handler unit. Therefore, in cooling mode, the automatic option might be preferable.

More sophisticated thermostats will display :

A message when the air handler filter must be cleaned or replaced. **The most frequent cause of heat pump problems is the failure to clean/change air filters.**

The stage the compressor is operating in (first stage..lower energy requirements or second stage...higher energy requirements) and whether auxiliary heat strips are active. This feature is very desirable because the stage that is active gives the homeowner an idea of how "hard' the heat pump is working to maintain setpoint. Operation in stage 1 most of the time is preferable because it is more efficient.
Aux. heat strips that are active in not-so-cold weather could be an indication of a system problem.

AUTO-RECOVERY allows the heating/cooling system to recover gradually from a thermostat setback, reducing the number of times auxiliary heat strips are activated.

5.7 MAINTENANCE OF HEAT PUMPS

In order to have a trouble-free heat pump, there are some basic tasks that must be performed on a regular basis. For the majority of systems, the **homeowner normally checks** just a few things:

A. The air filter (on water-to-air systems) should be cleaned or replaced monthly during the heating season, less frequently during the cooling season. There are electrostatic filters that can be cleaned; most other types have to be replaced.
B. The drain pan in the heat pump should be emptied and clean (with household bleach) monthly during the cooling season.

C. The settings and indicators on the thermostat and the heat pump unit should be checked periodically and if pressure and temperature measuring devices are installed, the readings recorded.

HVAC personnel normally are responsible for the following maintenance functions:

1.For a water-to-air system, the fan blades and the air coil within the air handler should be cleaned at least once a season.

2. Testing the input and output temperatures of the water in the ground loop . The two temperatures are known as **EWT** (Entering Water Temperature) and **LWT** (Leaving Water Temperature). The difference between these two temperatures, the **ground loop delta "T"** must be in a narrow range if the system is working properly. A range of 4-8 degrees F. is normal.

3. Testing the input(return) and output(supply) temperatures of the air in the duct system near the air handler (the **air handler delta "T"**) in a water-to-air system. A range of 20-30 degrees F. is normal.

4. Testing the difference between the input and output water temperatures of the desuperheater (the **desuperheater delta T**). Normally this is within about a 5 to 12 degree F. range.

5. Testing the voltage and amperage of the electrical components of the system, especially the current drawn by the compressor and air handler fan.

6. Testing the ground loop water pressure, with any necessary adjustment needed including adding any "make up" water/antifreeze. The antifreeze % should be checked and compared to specs.

7. The capacity of the electrical capacitor (in microfarads) in the compressor circuit should be measured.

The duct system's air flow **CFM** (cubic feet per minute) would be checked if there was a complaint of ineffective heating or cooling. It is more difficult to check so it would be done after the above tests are done and no cause of the problem was found. A **manometer** is used to check the air flow.

The refrigerant charge of the system should be tested as infrequently as possible, especially if there are no apparent problems with the system. The reason for this is that each time the servicemen attach their gauges to the refrigerant line, there is a loss of refrigerant. They may routinely add refrigerant each time to compensate for this but the result is usually that the system charge is not the correct system specification. Overcharging or undercharging the refrigerant lines is problematic.

5.8 HEAT PUMP PROBLEMS

Most modern ground source heat pumps have built-in protection to shut down the system if a serious problem is detected. This is called a **lockout**. Indicators on the unit will light up or flash to help identify the problem. The owner's manual should be used as a guide to identify these problems. The following is a list of the potential problems for any heat pump.

High Refrigerant Pressure heating mode	The homeowner can fix item 1. A service call is needed for all others.	1. Air Filter dirty 2. Air Coil dirty 3. Air blower malfunction 4. TXV malfunction 5. Refrigerant overcharge
Low Refrigerant Pressure heating mode	A service call is needed to correct all problems listed.	1. Loop water EWT too low 2. Loop water flow too low/ defective water pump 3. TXV malfunction 4. Air return temp too low 5. Refrigerant undercharge 6. Refrigerant leak
Loop Water Flow heating mode	A lockout will occur if the freeze protection thermistor encounters a loop water temperature that is too low. A service call is needed to correct all problems listed.	1. EWT too low 2. Flow pump malfunction 3. Restriction in loop/air in loop 4. Restriction in TXV 5. Low refrigerant charge 6. Freeze thermistor not set at proper temperature

High Refrigerant Pressure cooling mode	A service call is needed to correct all problems listed.	1. EWT too high 2. Entering air temp too high 3. Restricted loop water flow/ defective water pump 4. Flow pump malfunction 5. Restriction in TXV 6. Fouled heat exchanger
Low Refrigerant Pressure cooling mode	The homeowner can fix item 2. A service call is needed to correct all other problems listed.	1. Air Coil dirty 2. Air filter needs replacement 3. TXV restriction 4. Air flow too low 5. Return air temp too low 6. Refrigerant undercharge 7. Refrigerant leak
Air Flow	A lockout may occur if the fan speed in the air handler drops below a minimum rpm. A service call is needed to correct all problems listed.	1. Fan damaged or not spinning freely 2. Low supply voltage 3. Control board problem
Condensate Drain	The homeowner may be able to correct the problems listed	1. Plugged drain pan 2. Plugged drain line

If the system is in heating mode, the loop water temperature may have fallen below freezing (32 degrees F.). If there is no, or little, antifreeze in the system, a freeze-up condition may occur. The heat pump should automatically shut down with this condition. Three types of anti-freeze are used in the U.S. and Canada: propylene glycol, methyl alcohol and ethyl alcohol. The antifreeze used must be the one specified by the heat pump manufacturer. Verify with the serviceman that loop water has sufficient anti-freeze. Since the addition of antifreeze to the loop water decreases loop thermal conductivity and raises the flow rate required for turbulent flow, it is important that the amount of antifreeze added is not excessive. The following table can be used to estimate the amount of water in a loop. The amount of antifreeze needed can then be estimated, normally in the range of 15-20%.

HDPE Pipe Volume Capacity

Pipe Type	Nominal Size (inches)	Inner Diameter (inches)	Water volume (US gal/100ft)
SDR 11	3/4	0.86	3.0
	1	1.08	4.7
	1 1/4	1.36	7.5
	1 1/2	1.55	9.8
	2	1.94	15.4
	3	2.86	33.4
	4	3.69	55.4

Drain Pan Overflow

The drain pan is needed to collect any condensation that forms on the coil within the air handler when the system is in cooling mode. The drain pan should be checked and cleaned at least once a month during the cooling season. If it is necessary, a solution of water and household bleach can be used to clean the pan and the attached drain pipe. Some heat pumps will shut down if the pan is full. Therefore, if a homeowner is going to be away from home for any length of time, the drain pan should be checked prior to departure.

Misc.

In the event of an error condition that the system cannot correct as shown by the indicator lights when the heat pump is turned off, and then on again, call the serviceman. This is considered a "lock-out" condition and the system will automatically be placed in EMER (emergency) mode, turning the compressor off and relying on auxiliary electrical heat strips to provide (expensive) heat.

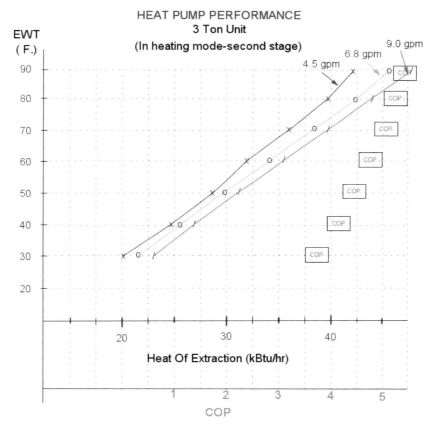

Figure 5.9.1

5.9 HEAT PUMP PERFORMANCE

The primary test for a heat pump is the measurement of **Heat of Extraction** (in heating mode) and **Heat of Rejection** (in cooling mode). Heat of extraction (**HE**) should be measured during the annual checkup of the geo-system. Heat of Extraction is the rate at which the heat pump is removing thermal energy from the ground loop. The measurement should be compared to the manufacturer's specifications. The measurement is in thousands of BTU/hour, the same units used for specifying the heating load. There are several variables which must be considered when the HE is evaluated because HE is not a constant. It is a variable and all of the following factors will determine its value at any instant in time; they are:

1. The water flow rate into, and therefore out of, the heat pump in gallons per minute (gpm).
2. Whether the heat pump's compressor is running in first or second stage.
3. The entering water temperature (EWT) as measured at water/refrigerant heat exchanger.
4. The airflow through the air handler in cubic feet per minute (cfm).

If all of these factors are known, the expected HE can be found in heating performance tables of the manufacturer's specifications. The actual HE can calculated by using the following formula:

HE= (EWT - LWT)   X   Water flow rate (in gpm)   X   Flow Factor

where **EWT - LWT**, the temperature difference between the entering and leaving water, in degrees Fahrenheit, is known as the **loop delta "T"**.

The **Flow Factor** (also known as the brine factor) is dependent on the amount and type of antifreeze used. The value of 450 is often used for antifreeze: 500 without antifreeze. For more precision, a table of values for different antifreeze mixtures is used. EWT and LWT are easy to measure if ports were installed on the ground loops to measure temperature and pressure, something which should always be done.

The water flow rate could be measured with a flow meter but is usually established based on pressure drop between the entering and leaving water. This is known as the **loop delta "P."** Using the heat pump's specifications, the variables of loop water entering temperature, pressure drop and whether the unit is running in partial or full load (i.e., the heat pump is running in stage 1 or stage 2), the water flow rate in gpm can be determined. The heat of extraction can then be calculated and compared to the value in the specifications.

Figure 5.9.1 is a graph displaying the relationship between HE, EWT and COP for a specific 3 ton heat pump. As would be expected, HE increases with both higher EWT and with an increased water flow rate. The same is true of COP, the heat pump's efficiency. The graph represents a heat pump running in second stage. If it were running in first stage, the efficiency (i.e., COP) would be higher due mainly to reduced compressor electrical consumption but the HE would be about 70% of that at second stage.

Heating Capacity (HC), the rate of total thermal energy delivered by the heat pump is the sum of heat of extraction (from the ground loop) and heat delivered from electrical devices (primarily the compressor and air handler fan). Its value, at any instant in time, is the sum of HE and of the sum of product of the voltage, current, the power factor (.85) and the constant 3.412 for the above mentioned electrical components. HC is measured in BTU/hr.

$$HC = HE + E \times I \times 3.412 \times .85$$

Although the heat pump performance graph is for a 3 ton unit, it should be pointed out that the range of heat of extraction, and therefore HC, can cover a wide range. The 3 ton unit, which one might expect to have a maximum HC or HE of 36,000 BTU/hr can have a higher maximum depending on EWT. The range of HC and HE for this 3-ton unit (in Full Load and 9 gpm flow rate) is shown in the table below:

Heat of Extraction/Heating Capacity for 3 ton heat pump (Full Load-9 gpm)

EWT (°F.)	20	30	40	50	60	70	80	90
HE (kBTU/hr)	18.7	22.7	26.8	30.9	35.1	39.4	43.9	48.5
HC (kBTU/hr)	26.2	30.4	34.8	39.3	43.9	48.7	53.7	58.8

The amount of heat contributed by the electrical components, primarily the compressor and air handler fan (i.e., HC-HE) is apparent from the table above. Since it is evident from this table that HC is a variable for any system, determined primarily by EWT (for a specific heat pump), the advice given in previous parts of this book has to be emphasized:

Make sure that the you are not short-looped. Adding some "fat" to the loop will benefit your system during extreme cold periods in heating dominated regions and during extreme hot periods in cooling dominated regions.

Slinky Loop Installation courtesy Palace Geothermal LLC

CHAPTER 6 THE HORIZONTAL GROUND LOOP

6.1 HORIZONTAL GROUND LOOP SYSTEMS

Ground loops are the conduits of heat to and from heat pumps. Using the terminology introduced in *Chapter 4- THE REFRIGERATOR*, ground loops function as both an evaporator (which absorbs heat) and a condenser (which dispenses heat).

The two broadest categories of closed ground loops are **water-source loop systems** and **DX (Direct eXchange) ground loop systems**. Water-source ground loops use water, and usually water and antifreeze, as the **working fluid** to transfer heat to and from the heat pump. DX systems use a refrigerant, just as the common refrigerator does, to transfer heat to and from the heat pump. At the current time, the preponderance of residential geo-systems are water-source systems. DX systems will be described in *Chapter 10*. The balance of this chapter will be devoted to horizontal, closed, water-source ground loop systems although some of the basic ground loop configurations apply to DX systems as well.

Water-source ground loops are almost always constructed from **High Density PolyEthylene (HDPE)** tubing due to its toughness and resistance to deterioration from chemicals. It is also flexible and can withstand sub-freezing temperatures without damage.

> **High density polyethylene tubing, HDPE (called "polypipe"),** normally a glossy black in color but sometimes green, is used in subsurface geothermal loops because of its strength, flexibility and chemical resistance. In general, there are two types used in residential geo-systems based on pressure ratings:
> SDR 11 (160psi at 73 degress F.)
> SDR 9 (200psi at 73 degrees F.)
> Poly pipe comes in 3/4", 1", 1 1/4", 2" (inside diameter)
> Cost is about $600 for a length of 500 feet.

Sections of **polypipe** can be welded together using a process called **heat fusion welding** without any loss of pipe strength. This requires a special tool called a fusion welding machine.

An example of a hand held fusion welding machine is shown on the following page.

Figure 6.1.1   Hand-held fusion welding machine   Courtesy McElroy Manufacturing Inc.

Horizontal ground loop systems are **closed-loop systems**. Closed-loop systems, as opposed to open-loop systems, circulate a fixed amount of **working fluid** within a loop system. The working fluid used in these systems is water or a mixture of water and antifreeze. There are several configurations of horizontal closed-loop systems, which will be described next, they are:

The **Straight Loop Configuration**.
The **Slinky Loop Configuration**.
The **Spiral Loop Configuration**.

Figure 6.2.1

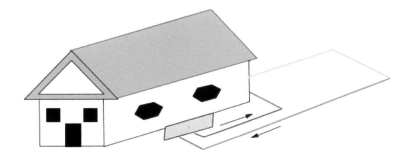

Straight, Single, Horiz. Loop

Table 6.2.1   Thermal-conductivity of Materials

Material	Conductivity (BTU/(hr-ft^2)($^\circ$F/ft)
Clay (dry to moist)	.087 - 1.04
Clay (saturated)	.35 - 1.45
Earth (dry)	.87
Granite	.98 - 2.31
Limestone	.73 - .77
Marble	1.2 - 1.7
Quartz (mineral)	1.73
Rock (solid)	1.16 - 4.05
Sand (dry)	.087 - .14
Sand (moist)	.14 - 1.16
Sand (saturated)	1.16 - 2.31
Sandstone	.98
Water	.34

6.2 THE STRAIGHT, SINGLE LOOP CONFIGURATION

Figure 6.2.1 is an illustration of the basic straight, single loop configuration which consists of a single, uninterrupted (i.e., no "T" connectors) section of polypipe. In residential applications 3/4 inch, SDR11, HDPE polypipe is most frequently used. Requiring a fairly large plot of land, the single length of polypipe is laid down in a trench excavated with a backhoe or trencher at a depth of four to eight feet. For extremes in climate, both hot and cold, the deeper the pipe should be buried and, at minimum, should be below the frost line of the local area.

When the polypipe is laid in the ground, it should be surrounded with material devoid of sharp stones to avoid damage from abrasion. Since the heat absorption and heat dispersion of the ground loop is highly dependent on the characteristics of the surrounding material, some thought should be given to which fill material is used. Table 6.2.1 lists the thermal conductivity of different materials. In general, materials that are able to retain moisture have higher thermal conductivity than those that dry out leaving gaps that might be filled with air. Therefore, if sand is used, fine grain sand rather than a course grade of sand is preferred. As the material is placed around the polypipe, layer by layer, it should be throughly soaked with a water hose so that no air pockets remain.

As shown in Figure 6.2.1, the basic straight, single loop configuration which, as its name implies, contains only a single loop. However, it is common to embed more than one loop in a trench. Sometimes, as many as 3 loops will be embedded in the same trench. This is known as a **6-pipe system** because at any section of the trench, there are 6 pipes that traverse that cross section. Most common are 2-pipe, 4-pipe and 6-pipe systems. If multiple loops are embedded in this configuration, a deeper trench is needed and the loops should be at least two feet apart.

For all horizontal ground loops, regardless of the type of configuration, the primary source of thermal energy is derived from solar radiation heating the top layers of the ground. When the loops extract heat from the surrounding ground, the replenishment of that heat, called **thermal recharge**, takes place from the surrounding ground, which obtains most of its thermal energy from the absorption of solar radiation and to a lesser extend, conduction from deeper earth. With this in mind, the following advice is offered:

In areas where heating is of primary concern, do not cover the ground above the horizontal loop with anything that will prevent the absorption of solar radiation, including anything that will cast a shadow over that area, especially when the sun is lower during the winter. In areas where cooling is of primary concern, do use planting of trees, shrubs, etc., to retard the absorption of solar energy by the ground as long as tree roots are kept away from the loops.

The length of polypipe needed for a particular heating/cooling load using a closed, straight ground loop is dependent on a number of factors including loop cross-sectional diameter, soil conductivity, loop depth and undisturbed underground temperature.

Figure 6.3.1

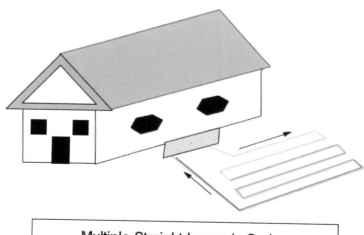

Multiple Straight Loops in Series

6.3 MULTIPLE, STRAIGHT LOOPS IN SERIES CONFIGURATION

Figure 6.3.1 on the previous page illustrates the multiple, straight loops in series configuration and is very similar to the basic single loop configuration. The only difference is that the single loop configuration is reconfigured into multiple, parallel loops and therefore requires, for the same loop length, a shorter but wider loop field. There is a minimum suggested separation of adjoining loops to allow for the thermal recharge of the surrounding ground. A minimum of 6 feet between loops is suggested.

The multiple, straight loops in series configuration is often implemented by excavating the entire area and laying the polypipe rather than excavating the individual loop trenches. In any closed, ground source, water-based system, there is a consideration that must always be taken into account. The water flow rate must be above a minimum gallons-per-minute rate to ensure adequate transfer of heat between the loop and the surrounding ground, and therefore, there are limits on the length of loops. The limitation incurred is due to the ever increasing power of the water pump required to maintain this minimum flow rate as the loop length is increased. This topic is addressed in section 6.8, *Turbulent Loop Flow And Reynolds Number*. In general, for closed loops, a flow rate in the range of 2.25 to 3 gallons per minute is the goal. If the loops are too long, the water pump(s) needed to maintain this flow rate will become larger and more expensive, both in installation and usage costs.

Figure 6.4.1

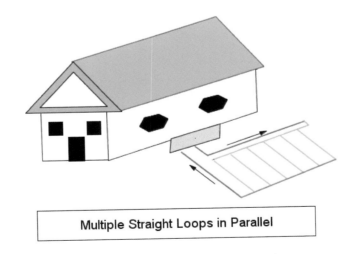

Multiple Straight Loops in Parallel

6.4 MULTIPLE, STRAIGHT LOOPS IN PARALLEL CONFIGURATION

Figure 6.4.1 on the previous page illustrates the multiple, straight loops in parallel configuration. This configuration differs from the prior two horizontal loop configurations in that there are multiple paths, or **circuits**, that the working fluid can take within the loop system. This structure may necessitate the addition of "T" section couplings for each loop circuit depending on how the circuits are connected together. **Heat fusion welding** is used to connect the sections of polypipe with the "T" connectors if the manifold is outside the residence. As with an electrical parallel circuit, the resistance to flow in each circuit is less in a parallel configuration than in a single loop configuration. Since this results in a lower flow rate in each circuit, the total number of circuits used is limited in number to provide the 2.25 to 3 gpm needed for turbulent flow in each circuit. Additionally, and more important, is the rate of heat absorption.

One of the basic concepts of thermodynamics is that the rate of heat transfer between two objects is directly proportional to their difference in temperatures. With a straight loop in the heating mode, the water flowing through the loop gradually gets warmer as it progresses through the loop. This means that the temperature differential between the water and the surrounding earth decreases as the water progresses through the loop resulting in a lower transfer rate near the end of the loop pipe. In each circuit of a parallel loop system, the water enters each circuit at its lowest temperature and therefore, a greater volume of water begins to absorb heat at the highest temperature differential, making this a more efficient configuration. Being a more efficient configuration means the total loop size can be smaller than a comparable single loop configuration.

It should be noted that the loop architecture in the illustration conforms to the desired **"reverse return plumbing"** concept when parallel circuits are used. Basically, this means that the total path length from the beginning of the loop to the end of the loop, through any parallel circuit, is the same length. This insures an equal flow rate through each circuit and results in a balanced system. Another consideration with parallel loops is that the water flow rate must be kept in a turbulent status (see 6.8 *Turbulent Loop Flow And Reynolds Number*) to attain maximum heat transfer between the loop and the earth.

Almost all water-source, closed loop geo-system heat pumps use a design water flow rate of about 2 to 3 gpm per ton of heat load capacity. When the loop field is designed, usually each circuit should have a maximum flow rate no greater than about 3 gpm. The reason for this is 3 gpm is usually more than sufficient for turbulent flow, which is necessary for optimum heat transfer between the ground and the loop without incurring excessive, and expensive, pumping power.

Figure 6.5.1

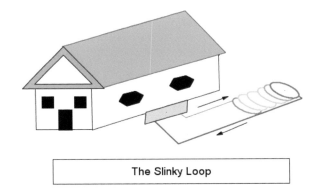

The Slinky Loop

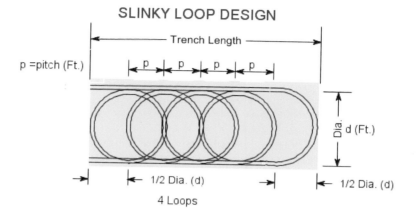

SLINKY LOOP DESIGN

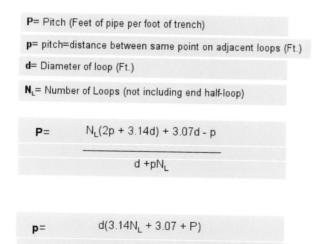

P= Pitch (Feet of pipe per foot of trench)

p= pitch=distance between same point on adjacent loops (Ft.)

d= Diameter of loop (Ft.)

N_L= Number of Loops (not including end half-loop)

$$P = \frac{N_L(2p + 3.14d) + 3.07d - p}{d + pN_L}$$

$$p = \frac{d(3.14N_L + 3.07 + P)}{N_L(P - 2) + 1}$$

Figure 6.5.2

6.5 THE SLINKY LOOP CONFIGURATION

Figure 6.5.1 on the previous page illustrates the basic Slinky configuration which is a single loop in which the polypipe is formed into a flat structure of overlapping circular rings which are usually, but not always, 3 feet in diameter. The Slinky configuration requires substantially more polypipe per foot of trench than most other configurations but the trench lengths are correspondingly shorter. Parallel circuits, each with a Slinky loop, are usually employed as shown in the phto at the beginning of this chapter.

There are two ways to embed the Slinky loops, either horizontal (laying flat at the bottom of the trench) or vertical (standing on end in the trench). The vertical installation uses a much narrower trench, which could be excavated by a trencher rather than a backhoe, but their heat transfer capability is about the same as the horizontal Slinky. There is a concern that vertical Slinky loops might trap air at the top of the loops, impeding water flow through them. This is a good reason to make sure that the loops are thoroughly purged of air when they are installed, although purging is a must for all closed ground loops. After the loop is installed, a powerful water pump, attached to a **purge cart**, is used to force all air out of the loop circuits. The amount of overlap of each succeeding loop in a Slinky configuration is determined by the pitch used. **Pitch**, when applied to Slinky loops can have two different meanings:

1. More often, it is used to indicate the distance (in inches) from one point on a circular ring to the corresponding point on an adjacent circular ring. This will be referred to as "**p**" in Figure 6.5.2.

2. The second definition of pitch is the number of linear feet of polypipe in one linear foot of trench. This will be referred to as "**P**" in Figure 6.5.2.

This dual definition of pitch can lead to confusion in the interpretation of a loop design. The first definition might be expressed, for example, as "A 12-inch pitch Slinky." The second definition would be expressed, for example, as "A 10-Pitch Slinky."

The first definition (p) is useful when constructing the Slinky loops but the second definition (P) is more meaningful because it specifies exactly how much polypipe per linear foot of trench is present, regardless of the diameter of the loop used. This readily allows comparison of Slinky loops to other configurations on a trench-length-per-ton of heat/cooling basis (see Figure 6.7.1). A 12-Pitch Slinky loop, using the second definition would have a different structure than a loop with a 12 inch pitch even if the loop diameters were the same. Figure 6.5.2 includes a formula which shows the relationship between the variables of a Slinky loop. Therefore, the homeowner should understand which usage of "pitch" is being specified in the installation contract. Slinky loops can either be pre-formed and shipped to the installation site or formed at that location.

The trench length for a Slinky is much less than a comparable straight, single loop (i.e., a 2- pipe) system (of the same tonnage). For example, a 10-Pitch Slinky (per the second definition of pitch), 3 feet in diameter with a 3/4 inch inner pipe diameter, used in an area where the undisturbed underground temperature is 52 degrees F. (at a depth of 5 feet) would require a trench that was 115 feet long per ton of heating/cooling load. This translates to a total of 1150 linear feet of pipe per ton. For a single loop (i.e., a 2-pipe system) needed to satisfy the same load, a 250 foot long trench/ton would be required, resulting in a pipe loop length of 500 linear feet per ton. See section 6.7 *Sizing A Closed Horizontal Ground Loop* for more detailed information. There is a limit to the amount of pipe that should be used in a single Slinky circuit, which is in the 1000-1600 foot range, depending on pipe diameter. As noted earlier, more powerful, expensive pumps become necessary when the loop lengths are increased. Another factor that comes into play is known as turbulent flow and will be addressed later. Slinky loops with a high Pitch (based on the second definition of pitch) are often referred to as a **"compact Slinky"** and can reduce the overall trench length by over 2/3 compared to a simple two-pipe loop.

> **RULE OF THUMB FOR SLINKY LOOPS is that the there should be at least 8-12 linear feet of pipe in 1 foot of trench length. This would be referred to as an 8-Pitch to 12-Pitch Slinky.**
> **Total Slinky loop length/ton is generally 800-1000 Ft./ton for 3/4 inch pipe.**

Since the Slinky configuration is employed over a much smaller footprint than non-Slinky configurations, there is a lower thermal content of the enclosed volume of ground and the possibility of **ground thermal depletion** is high. This could be a problem in either a very high heating or very high cooling environment. Therefore, it is important to make sure the size of the loop field is not shortchanged. Also, the recommended spacing between Slinky loops is 8 to 12 feet but this guideline is often ignored. As a result, **thermal depletion/recharge** may be a problem when this guideline is not followed or extra loop not added.

The concept of **"deeper is better"** when referring to the depth at which loops should be buried is especially true for Slinky loops. With a much smaller volume of the ground to extract/inject heat, the possibility of thermal depletion is much higher for Slinky loops, especially in extremely hot or extremely cold locations. Therefore, **deeper excavation for Slinky loops is preferred**.

6.6 THE SPIRAL LOOP CONFIGURATION

Figure 6.6.1 illustrates the basic Spiral configuration which is similar to that of the Slinky. The difference is that the circular loops are not flattened; they form a cylinder. This configuration is less common in both the USA and Europe because of the additional work needed to form the spiral, set it in the trench and carefully backfill the trench. The Spiral configuration is more efficient than the Slinky, because the ground "envelope" enclosed by the spiral is larger and permits greater thermal recharge capability. It would require a shorter trench than a comparable (i.e., same tonnage) Slinky loop but would have to be set in a trench that was deeper by an amount equal to the loop diameter.

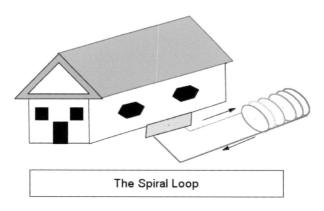

The Spiral Loop

Figure 6.6.1

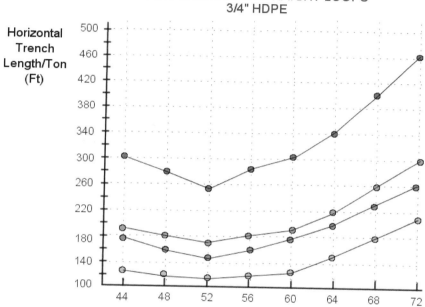

Figure 6.7.1

6.7 SIZING A CLOSED HORIZONTAL GROUND LOOP

One of the most challenging tasks of a residential, geothermal system designer is to design a loop field of the proper size. Unlike the heat pump size determination, which can be deduced from the heating/cooling load, the loop field is harder to design. The heat pump size (i.e., tonnage) can be determined from a Manual-J calculation or other method where known data is available. Not so for a loop field for a variety of reasons.

> **For each trench used in a water-source, horizontal, ground closed loop system, the trench length-per-ton of heating/cooling capacity for a specific size (i.e., cross section diameter) of loop pipe is determined by four factors:**
> **1. The conductivity (k) of the surrounding ground.**
> **2. The depth at which the loop is buried.**
> **3. The loop structure (i.e., slinky, straight/# pipes, etc.).**
> **4. The average undisturbed, underground temperature at the location.**

Figure 6.7.1 is a graph displaying the Trench Length per ton vs. the Average Ground Temperature for several different horizontal loop configurations. The graph assumes a loop pipe of $3/4$ inch HDPE buried 5 feet below ground with a ground conductivity (k) of 0.6 Btu/hr-ft-degree F. To obtain a more accurate trench size/ton based on different ground conductivities, select one of the following multiplier factors based on the appropriate conductivity:

Multiplier Factor for Ground Conductivity

Ground Conductivity (Btu/hr-ft-degree F.)	Multiplier Factor
0.4	1.22
0.6	1.00
0.8	0.89
1.0	0.82

Multiply the trench length (ft.)/ton obtained from the first graph by the Multiplier Factor from the table above to obtain the revised total trench length(ft.)/ton. As an example, to estimate the total trench length needed for a 4 ton heating load, located in an area where the average ground temperature is 60 degrees F., ground conductivity of 0.6BTU/hr-ft -degree F. and a 10-pitch $^3/_4$ inch Slinky is planned to be used, the graph indicates the following:

Horizontal trench length per ton required is 125 feet/ton. The 4 ton system could be served with 5-100 foot trenches, each with 10-Pitch Slinky loops, connected in parallel to accommodate the system. Each trench would require 1000 linear feet of polypipe for a total length of 5000 feet. Using 6-9 shorter trenches would lower pumping costs significantly but the minimum flow rate necessary for turbulent flow must be considered.

From the graph it can be seen that the shortest trench needed occurs in areas where the average undisturbed ground temperature is in the 52 to 55 degree F. range. In these areas the demand for combined heating and cooling is at a minimum. Southern regions, where the underground temperatures are very high, require the highest trench length/ton, for cooling. In cooling mode, the system must not only dissipate the heat from the residence's interior, it must also reject heat produced by the heat pump's compressor and the air handler's fan. When the heat pump runs in heating mode, the above two sources of heat supplement the heat extracted from the ground loop.

TRENCH LENGTH PER TON for closed, horizontal ground loops extends over a wide range, from a minimum of 120 feet/ton for a 10-Pitch Slinky configuration to at least 460 feet/ton for a straight 2-pipe loop configuration using 3/4 inch HDPE. The loop configuration is the primary factor. Local undisturbed underground temperatures have the next biggest impact on trench length/ton, followed by geological conditions, such as subsurface content: sand, clay, soil and moisture. Always estimate on the high side for ground loop length to avoid costly re-excavation costs for an undersized ground loop.

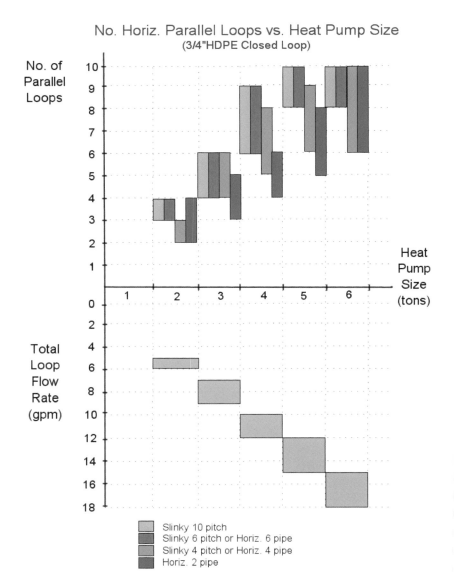

No. Horiz. Parallel Loops vs. Heat Pump Size
(3/4"HDPE Closed Loop)

No. of Parallel Loops

Heat Pump Size (tons)

Total Loop Flow Rate (gpm)

Slinky 10 pitch
Slinky 6 pitch or Horiz. 6 pipe
Slinky 4 pitch or Horiz. 4 pipe
Horiz. 2 pipe

Figure 6.7.3

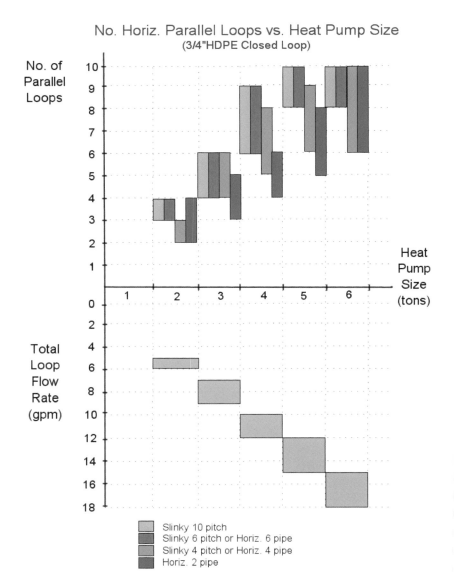

106

Once the total loop trench length is calculated for the system, the decision has to be made as to the number of parallel circuits (i.e., trenches) to be used. There is some flexibility in deciding the number of circuits to be used, which might be influenced by the configuration of land around the residence. The graph in Figure 6.7.3 can be used as a guide for selecting the number of circuits based on the system's heat pump capacity. Also, an estimate of the range of total water flow rate (to/from the heat pump) can be found at the bottom of the graph. As noted, this total water flow rate should be distributed equally among all the circuits. The heat pump manufacturer's specification for water flow rate should be adhered to.

From the graph , depending on the size of the heat pump, it can be seen that the **maximum number of parallel circuits per ton** (up to 6 tons) can be up to 2 1/4 and the **minimum number of parallel circuits per ton** is 1. If the maximum number of circuits as specified in the graph is used, there could be a problem maintaining turbulent flow in the circuits.

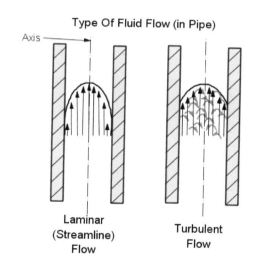

Type Of Fluid Flow (in Pipe)

Axis

Laminar
(Streamline)
Flow

Turbulent
Flow

Figure 6.8.1   **Figure 6.8.2**

6.8 LOOP TURBULENT FLOW AND REYNOLDS NUMBER

Within a closed ground loop in a geo-system, either vertical or horizontal, water with antifreeze is pumped throughout the enclosed loop circuit. This is, using fluid mechanics terminology, a forced flow. Forced flow of a fluid, water in this instance, can be in a **laminar** state, a **turbulent** state or a transitional mode between the two states.

At low velocity, laminar flow exists. When the flow is laminar, all sections of the fluid move in paths that are parallel to the axis of the tube, or pipe, through which the fluid is moving. Squeezing an uncapped toothpaste tube, for example, will result in a laminar flow of toothpaste out of the tube. In an HDPE pipe that is buried below ground and has water pumped through it, there is a transfer of thermal energy between the water and the surrounding ground. Under these conditions a true laminar flow cannot occur because there are convection currents resulting from the temperature differential between the water/ground. The result is a modified laminar flow which is technically described as a **non-isothermal** laminar flow. The meaning of non-isothermal is: not at constant temperature. Within a laminar or modified laminar flow, heat transfer between the water and the surrounding ground is minimized because most of the water flowing through the pipe will not pass near the inner surface of the pipe to transfer thermal energy to the pipe. In fact, a graph of the water velocity vs. position within the pipe will be a parabolic curve; Figure 6.8.1 illustrates this. In a laminar flow the highest flow rate is along the tube's axis. This means that at any point directly next to the pipe's inner surface, the water velocity will be zero. Moving toward the center of the pipe, the velocity increases and is at a maximum at the center of the pipe. It then decreases again as the position moves to the opposite surface of the pipe where velocity again falls to zero. This produces an average flow rate that is 50% of the maximum (along the axis) flow rate.

To achieve high thermal transfer between the water and the pipe, and therefore the surrounding ground, the water velocity must be increased until a turbulent flow is achieved. When this happens, the average water molecule flowing in the pipe no longer follows a path parallel to the pipe's wall but moves forward in a more random pattern because of eddy currents where it is much more likely to move closer to the pipe's inner wall and transfer more thermal energy to it. The turbulent flow pattern illustrated in Figure 6.8.2 displays a more flattened parabolic movement of the flow where the water flow closer to the tube's wall is moving faster compared to laminar flow and with more eddy current formation. This results in greater thermal transfer.

The degree of turbulence of water flowing through an HDPE pipe can be associated with a dimension-less number known as the **Reynolds Number (R_e)**. Usually a Reynolds Number of 2300 is used as the cutoff between laminar and turbulent flows. However, a more precise definition is:

R_e less than 2000 is a laminar flow.
R_e between 2000 and 4000 is a transitional flow; meaning simultaneous laminar, turbulent flows could exist in this range.
R_e greater than 4000 is a turbulent flow.

The formula for calculating the Reynolds Number is:

$R_e = DVp/u$ Where D is the pipe inner diameter in feet
V is the average fluid velocity in feet per second
p is fluid density in pounds per cubic foot
u is the viscosity in pounds per foot-second. The viscosity is a measure of the "stickiness" of a fluid, i.e., the higher the viscosity, the greater resistance to flow.
In order to find the fluid velocity (V) for a specific Reynolds Number (Re), we solve the above equation for the fluid velocity:

$V = R_e u/Dp$

For closed ground loops, a total heat pump water flow rate of 3 gpm per ton of heat pump capacity is recommended with a minimum flow rate of 2.25 gpm per ton necessary for turbulent flow.

As an example, to find the water flow velocity in an HDPE pipe with 1 inch interior diameter necessary for turbulent flow, at a Reynolds Number of 4000, we would calculate as follows:

$V = R_e u/Dp = (4000)(1.546 \text{ centipoise} \times 0.0006672)/(.0833 \text{ ft})(62.4 \text{lb/ft}^3)$

NOTE: the Absolute-Dynamic Viscosity(u) is measured in centipoise (cp) and its value varies based on the temperature of the fluid. In this example, the viscosity value is used for water at 40 degrees F. To convert centipoise to pounds/ft-sec, multiply by .0006672.

Calculating the velocity needed:

V(velocity)=0.794 feet per second (needed for turbulent flow of water (at 40 degrees F.) in a HDPE pipe with a 1 inch interior diameter.

Converting this figure to cubic feet per second by finding the volume of a cylinder one inch in diameter and 0.794 ft long:

flow volume/sec = cross-sectional area of cylinder X cylinder length
$$= (pi)r^2 \quad x \quad 0.794$$
$$=(3.14)(.0417)^2 \quad x \quad 0.794$$
$$= .004164 \text{ ft}^3/\text{sec}$$
flow volume/minute = flow volume/sec x 60 =0.2498 ft^3/min

knowing that one cubic foot = 7.48 gallons
flow volume/minute = (0.2498)(7.48)= 1.866 gpm

Note that the above calculation indicates a minimum flow rate of 1.866 gallons per minute of pure water (without antifreeze) is required for turbulent flow in the pipe size and temperature specified. Since antifreeze increases the viscosity of water, its addition will influence the flow velocity needed for turbulent flow. Specifically, it would require a higher flow rate than that calculated for pure water. Antifreeze also deceases the thermal capacity and the thermal conductivity of the water.

As the flow rate in a pipe rises, the corresponding Reynolds Number increases and the rate of thermal transfer increases. However, the pressure drop also increases with increasing flow rates resulting in greater electrical cost to pump the water at the higher velocity. Therefore, there is a tradeoff between a higher thermal transfer rate and electrical pumping costs. Heat pump manufacturers' specifications list the optimum water flow rates in their ground loops. Typically, for water loops, a figure of 3 gallons per minute per ton of heating capacity is usually recommended. The following table illustrates the flow rates necessary to maintain turbulent flow in common geo-system pipe sizes.

Table 6.8.1   Reynolds Number for Various Pipe Sizes and Flow Rates With Pure Water

Pipe Size Diameter (inches)	Flow Rate (gpm)	Reynolds Number
3/4	1.59	3566
3/4	1.74	3904
3/4	1.9	4279
3/4	2.1	4617
3/4	3.0	6757
1	1.9	3453
1	2.1	3704
1	2.2	4004
1	2.4	4303
1	2.7	4855
1	3.0	5455
1 1/4	2.5	3441
1 1/4	2.7	3628
1 1/4	2.9	3816
1 1/4	3.0	4066
1 1/4	3.2	4254
1 1/4	4.8	6381

There are a few things that complicate the calculation of turbulent loop water flow rate. The viscosity (u) will vary based on the water temperature and the % of antifreeze used. In the example given, the (Absolute-Dynamic) viscosity of 1.546 for 40 degrees F. was used. Based on the information in the following table, it can be seen that the viscosity can vary by a factor up to 2.5 between water temperatures of 32-90 degrees F.

Variance in Water Viscosity based on Temperature

Temp. In degrees F.	Temp. In degrees C.	Viscosity (Absolute-Dynamic) in centipoise
32	0	1.794
40	4.4	1.546
50	10.0	1.310
60	15.6	1.129
70	21.1	0.982
80	26.7	0.862
90	32.2	0.764
100	37.8	0.682

Based on the above table, in colder climates where underground temperature surrounding loops can drop significantly, sometimes into the 20s (F.), water flow rates must not be near the minimum necessary for turbulent flow if optimum thermal transfer is expected. The percentage of antifreeze used will affect the calculation of turbulent flow rates. Antifreeze increases the viscosity of the mixture while lowering the thermal conductivity and the thermal capacity (i.e., the specific heat). As the % antifreeze is increased, the corresponding flow rate might have to be increased to reach the required Reynolds Number needed for turbulent flow.

6.9 HORIZONTAL LOOP BORING

It is not always necessary to fully excavate a site with trenches to install a ground loop. For non-Slinky-type straight loops, there are various tools that will bore tunnels below ground with little disturbance to the surface. There are various names for the procedures and equipment available to accomplish this boring; "**Moling**" is one such name. Basically, at both ends of the intended loop tunnel, a hole is dug that is large enough to accommodate the worker and the drill. The worker drills horizontally using the pneumatic tool to bore a tunnel to the other hole at the end of the loop field. The polypipe is then pulled through the tunnel. This method is often used to install pipe below driveways, sheds and other structures that might be a problem for conventional excavation. Although I don't recommend that the internal, heat pump equipment installation should be a Do-It-Yourself project, the loop installation might be for a simple loop configuration. Figure 6.9.1 is a drawing of horizontal drilling equipment.

Figure 6.9.1 Horizontal drilling   Courtesy Grundomat PTY LTD.

It is possible to install a straight loop as deep as 12 feet below the surface using this method? The walls of the deep pits would have to be structurally reenforced to protect the drillers from a cave-in. When loops are installed by excavating either for a trench or wide loop field, the area has to be backfilled. It takes months for the backfilling to be fully compacted, removing any air between the ground and the loops. Therefore, the COP, the efficiency, of the system will be lowered until the compaction has taken place. Horizontal drilling implementation of ground loops would mitigate this post-implementation lowering of COP to a certain extent.

6.10 USE OF A DRIP HOSE ON A LOOP FIELD

The conductivity of soil is greatly enhanced by the addition of moisture. Where temperatures are high and dry conditions are prevalent, **soaker hoses** or drip hoses are frequently placed on or below the surface above the ground loops. In areas where below freezing temperatures are experienced, the soaker hose must be buried beneath the frost line.Sometimes the depressed area created after loop installation is purposely not leveled with surrounding ground to provide a low point for accumulation of rain water for the purpose enhancing moisture in the loop field. This can be effective in warmer climates but can be counterproductive in colder climates. Frozen water and snow above the ground loop will eventually melt and deliver "ice cold" water to the loops, temporarily lowering their COP.

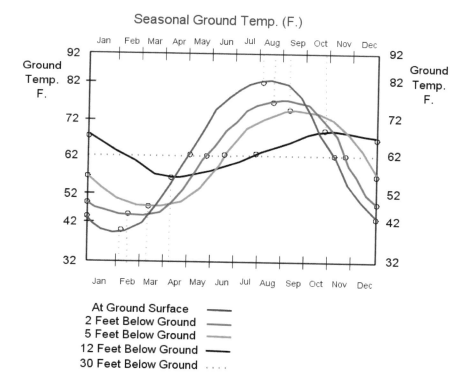

Figure 6.11.1

Throughout the year the temperature of the earth, down to about 30 feet, undergoes a gradual change as shown in the Figure 6.11.1. There is a wave-like rising and falling of the ground temperature throughout the four seasons, the intensity of which depends on the depth. For horizontal loops, there is a "flywheel effect", meaning the underground earth temperature will continue to rise after the summer peak in air temperature has been reached and starts to cool down. A comparable effect in the winter also occurs, i.e., the ground temperature continues to drop as the outside air attains its low temperature and starts to warm as can be seen in the chart. It should be noted that the chart represents the undisturbed subterranean temperature distribution. The presence of ground loops will cause greater fluctuations of the amplitude of the curves. It is not unusual, in the summer, to have loop water temperatures of 90 degrees F. in southern regions. Similarly, during the winter in northern regions, loop water temperatures of 25 to 30 degrees F. are not uncommon.

The chart also illustrates the changing pattern of temperature based on underground depth. The patterns at ground level, 2 feet below, 5 feet below, 12 feet below and 30 feet below can be seen. Although the chart represents temperatures in a region of moderate climate, the general shape of the chart is valid for regions with more extreme temperatures. The average ground (surface) temperatures of various cities are shown *Appendix A*.

Antifreeze
Antifreeze is necessary in geothermal ground loops, particularly if near-loop ground temperatures are expected to fall below 45 degrees F. The three classes of antifreeze are:

SALTS: Calcium Chloride and Sodium Chloride

GLYCOLS: Ethylene Glycol and Propylene Chloride

ALCOHOLS: Ethyl, Methyl and Isopropyl

The three most commonly used types of antifreeze are:

Propylene glycol (safest), Methanol (most toxic) and Ethylene glycol (moderately safe)
The glycols allegedly become gel-like at very low temperatures.

The main question involves the quantity (i.e., %) of antifreeze that should be used and this depends on the average, undisturbed ground temperature of the region and the loop configuration. For propylene-type antifreeze solutions:

% of Antifreeze Needed Based on Loop Type and Undisturbed Ground Temp.

Loop Config.	Pitch (linear len. in feet/ft-trench)	% of volume for temp 60-63 F.	% of volume for temp 52-59 F.	% of volume for temp 44-51 F.
Slinky	10 ft/ft	10	15	20
Slinky or Straight 6-pipe	6 ft/ft	10	15	20
Straight 2-pipe	2 ft/ft	10	15	20

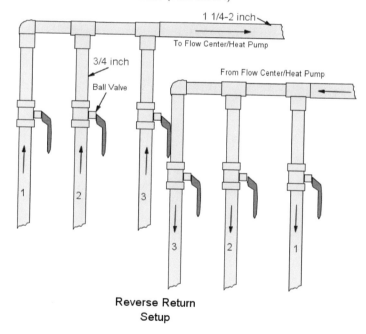

Figure 6.12.1

6.12 LOOP HEADERS AND MANIFOLDS

When there is more than one horizontal loop circuit, the loop pipes must be connected such that there is only a single pair of pipes that enter the heat pump. The transition from multiple circuits to a single pair of larger pipes takes place at a **manifold**, as shown in Figure 6.12.1. This pair of larger pipes is called a **header**, and sometimes a **lineset,** although "lineset" is usually used to reference refrigeration lines. The manifold can be located within the residence or buried underground. If underground, the manifold can be placed in a box-like protective concrete enclosure, a **vault**, or simply buried below earth. The boxed enclosure is preferable because it permits relatively easy access for maintenance.

All configurations of parallel loops, whether straight or slinky, for example, can have their circuits extend into the home's basement and connected at that point to a manifold. Locating the manifold indoors has the advantage of being able to attach equipment to monitor the temperature and pressure of each loop circuit, a distinct advantage if a problem arises. Although leaks in the underground loops are not common, an interior manifold would permit the leaking loop to be temporarily bypassed, allowing the system to continue to operate, at a lower performance level. The interior manifold configuration would incur additional expense due to the increase in loop pipe needed and the drilling of additional holes in the home's foundation.

Two manifolds are needed, one for the output leg of the loop structure and one for the input leg. Manifolds can be made of HDPE piping or the more durable, and expensive, brass. Manifolds can be either pre-fabricated or, in the case of HDPE, fabricated on-site. Figure 6.12.1 illustrates a manifold for a three circuit loop of 3/4 inch polypipe. Ball-valves should be used to isolate each circuit and to balance the flow in the all loops. Not shown are temperature/pressure gauges or ports for the purpose of monitoring loop conditions. However, the additional expense for this equipment is well worth it. The concept of "**reverse return**" is illustrated. Each circuit in a multi-circuit loop configuration should be as close to the same length as possible to have a balanced system.

6.13 LOOP FLOW CENTER

The **flow center** is the name given to the small unit where the two consolidated input and output ground loops, the **headers**, are connected to 1 or 2 flow pumps. Two pumps are common; one to pump water to the ground loop and another pump to pump the water from the ground loop to the heat pump. In general, a heat pump with a rating of 3 tons or less will have one pump; greater than 3 tons will have two pumps.

The flow center unit has connectors that allow the loops to be purged of air and filled with water/antifreeze. Common antifreeze solutions are methanol, propylene glycol and ethylene glycol. Flow centers are made of cast iron or brass. Usually instruments to measure the temperature of the water entering the flow center (EWT) and leaving the flow center (LWT) as well as gauges to measure the corresponding water pressures are positioned on the flow center. Figure 6.13.1 is a photo of a flow center. "**Pete's ports**" are pipe fittings that allow temperature and pressure gauges to be temporarily inserted unto the water loops. The size of the water pumps needed is based on the size (in tons) of the heat pump:

Size (and number) of Water Pumps Needed for Ground Loops

Heat Pump size	2 ton	3 ton	4 ton	5 ton	6 ton
Header size 1 ½ inch	(1) 1/12hp	(1) 1/6hp	(1) 1/6hp	(2) 1/6hp	(2) 1/6hp
Header size 1 1/4 inch	same	same	(2) 1/12hp	same	same

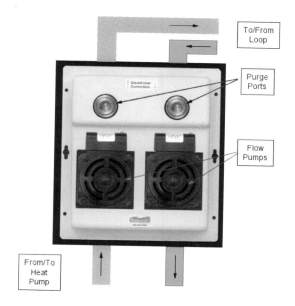

Figure 6.13.1 Flow Center

6.14 POND LOOPS

Pond loops are similar to horizontal, closed ground loops. Instead of being buried below ground, they are floated in a pond to their intended location, weighted down and sunk to the bottom. The pond, or lake, must be of sufficient size to act as a heat sink. One half acre per ton of heating/cooling load with a minimum depth of 8 feet is required. There are two configurations of loops commonly used:

1. The **Slinky/Matt Configuration** consists of a flat, "compact Slinky" around which is placed a thick plastic grid mat. The mat is used to protect the loops from being damaged by the weights which are attached to sink the Slinky loops. This configuration is the preferred one for use in heating dominated regions. The greater exposure of the individual loops to circulating water makes it a better heat sink.
2. The **Coiled Pond Loop Configuration** consists of a series of concentrically wound spiral loops with the bottom loop having the largest diameter and the top loop the smallest diameter but large enough to allow vertical water circulation within the spiral. This configuration is used in regions of more moderate climate.

Both loop configurations should be structured using reverse return plumbing. The loops should not rest directly on the bottom. They should be supported about two feet above the bottom to allow water circulation around all loops. Sufficient weighting of the loops to prevent the loops from floating to the surface is mandatory. There are several factors that increase buoyancy. The HDPE pipe material, the antifreeze within the pipe, air bubbles that might find their way into the pipe and ice that might form around the loops. When the pond is covered with thick ice and the loops float up beneath the ice, the remedy has been to stretch weighted chain link fencing on the ice above the loops and await the melting of the ice.

When a pond freezes over, the temperature at the pond bottom is about 39°F with a gradual temperature gradient up to the surface ice at 32°F. This occurs because water is at its highest density at 39°F, at which point it sinks to the bottom. This is what makes pond loops a viable, and cheaper, alternative to underground loops. An EWT near 39°F for a heat pump is considered good. A problem occurs when thermal energy is withdrawn from the loop at too fast a rate and the LWT drops below 32°F allowing the pond water surrounding the loop to freeze. This not only increases the buoyancy of the loops but also reduces the near-loop temperatures from 39°F to 32°F, lowering the effectiveness of the loop.In order to prevent this from happening there are two factors that the homeowner should consider in addition to adding additional weight to prevent the loops from floating:

1. A larger loop would reduce the chances of near-loop freezing of water. Standard practice is to install 300 feet per ton of piping for pond loops. Increasing the loop length per ton to at least 350 ft/ton would help.

2. Avoid thermostat setback. Setbacks cause the heat pump to work overtime to recover, and in so doing, lower near-loop temperatures excessively.

The freeze-over of ponds in northern regions is desirable because it insures that the pond bottom temperature will stabilize at 39°F. Anything that might mix the pond water, such as aeration devices, should be disabled during the winter.

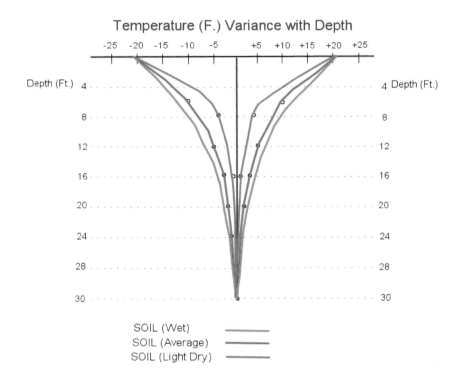

Figure 7.1.1

CHAPTER 7   THE VERTICAL GROUND LOOP

7.1 VERTICAL LOOP BASICS

Closed, vertical, water-based ground loops are placed in boreholes drilled approximately 4 to 6 inches in diameter and usually 150 to 400 feet deep. They are the main alternative to a closed horizontal loop system. Often, but not always, the choice of using vertical loops is made because there is insufficient land square footage for a horizontal loop field. On average, vertical, water-based loops require 100-300 square feet of land area per ton as opposed to 1000-2000 square feet per ton of horizontal loops, although these ranges can vary considerably based on the spacing between adjacent loops and the loop configuration.

Many of the considerations for closed, vertical, ground heat exchange loops are the same as for closed horizontal loops. It is strongly recommended that *Chapter 6* be read prior to this chapter. Drilling boreholes for vertical ground loops is much more expensive than excavating horizontal loop trenches. Large well-drilling rigs are a necessity and they are not cheap. Some of these rigs cost several hundred thousand dollars.They usually charge on a per foot of borehole drilled per well, often as high as $15 per foot to $23 per foot. Prices vary by region of the country and the degree of competition among well drillers. Some drillers will charge based on the tonnage of the system being installed. In this instance, expect to pay drilling costs of $2000 to $4000 per ton for the system installed. It is important for the homeowner to ask, when estimates are received, how the drilling costs are calculated and how firm the estimate is.

Seasonal variations in subterranean temperatures decrease as depth increases, unlike conditions in horizontal trenches. Figure 7.1.1 illustrates the depth variation of temperature in a region comparable to the northeast USA. This diminution of temperature variation by depth permits a shorter length of polypipe per ton compared to horizontal loops.

A rule of thumb for closed, vertical borehole loops, using 3/4 inch polypipe is that a minimum length of 300 feet of pipe (i.e. a borehole depth of 150 feet) per ton of heat transfer load is needed. It is recommended however, that in colder regions, at least 360 feet per ton (i.e., a borehole depth of 180 feet) be used to keep the entering water temperature (EWT) above 32 degrees F. In hotter regions, borehole depths of 200-250 ft./ton should be used.

The geology of the area where vertical boreholes are drilled will affect the efficiency (COP) of the system. The following table illustrates the conductivity and diffusivity of various subsurface materials.

THERMAL CONDUCTIVITY OF SUB-SURFACE MATERIALS

Soil Type	Conductivity	Diffus.	Description	Occurrence
Dense rock	2.00	.05	Dense/wet granite, limestone, quartzite	rare
Average rock	1.40	.04	Typical granite, limestones, sandstone	very common
Saturated sand/gravel	1.44	.036	Sand/gravel, static water table(70% loop)	common
Saturated silt/clay	0.96	.025	Silt/clay, static water table(70% loop)	somewhat rare

Damp sand/gravel	0.90	.027	Sand&gravel, water table <30% loop	rare
Damp silt/clay	0.75	.025	Silt/clay, static water table <30% loop	somewhat rare
Dry sand/gravel	0.35	.018	Sand/gravel minimum moisture	extremely rare
Dry silt/clay	0.50	.02	Silt/clay minimum moisture	extremely rare

Conductivity is the rate at which heat is transferred through a unit area of material per unit linear distance (at right angles) per degree of temperature gradient. Conductivity units are in thousands of BTU/hr- ft-degrees F.

Diffusivity is related to conductivity and is the rate that a temperature discontinuity propagates through a substance. A metal such as silver has a very high diffusivity. It is calculated by dividing its conductivity by the product of its density and its specific heat.

For larger geothermal installations, especially commercial ones, a thermal conductivity test of the ground is made in order to more accurately determine the number of boreholes needed, and their respective depths, to prevent expensive and inefficient oversizing and troublesome "**short looping.**" Due to the expense of this testing, which requires a borehole to be drilled to perform the testing, smaller residential installations omit this step. Because of this, most residential installers of vertical loop systems can only estimate the borehole field size based on their experience from installations in the locale of the new installation. **The ground thermal conductivity test consists of drilling a borehole, installing a loop and then** filling the loop with hot water. A data recording device logs the changes in temperature of the water in the loop over a 48 hour period. From this data, the borehole conductivity and diffusivity can be calculated.

The following chart demonstrates the wide range in cost and borehole size needed for a 10 ton vertical borehole installation based on a variation of ground thermal conductivity (of a minimum of .55 and maximum of 1.5). The estimates in drilling cost are also shown for 2 different drilling rates. Also note that this is a commercial-size installation, two to three times the average residential installation.

VARIATION IN BOREHOLE SIZE & COST BASED ON GROUND CONDUCTIVITY

Subsurface thermal conductivity (k)	# of U tubes...1 tube per borehole	Borehole depth X 2=loop length (ft)	Total U-tube length (ft)	U tube length per ton (ft)	Est. Cost based on $15/vert. ft	Est. Cost based on $9/vert. ft	Cost/ton @$15/ft/ @$9/ft
.55	16	199	3180	318	$47,710	$28,620	$4771/$2862
0.7	15	188	2820	282	$42,308	$25,380	$4231/$2538
0.85	14	187	2620	262	$39,308	$23,580	$3931/$2358
1.0	12	202	2420	242	$36,307	$21,780	$3631/$2178
1.2	12	188	2250	225	$33,757	$20,250	$3376/$2025
1.35	12	180	2160	216	$32,406	$19,440	$3241/$1944
1.5	10	212	2110	211	$31,656	$18,990	$3166/$1899

Note: The thermal conductivity (k) is measured in BTU per hour-foot- degree F.

It can be seen from the above table that for this 10 ton system, the subsurface conductivity can have a significant impact on the cost of the installation of the vertical ground loops:

At a drilling cost of $9/vertical-ft.....$9,630 difference between ground with maximum conductivity vs. min. conductivity.

At a drilling cost of $15/ vertical-ft...$16,054   difference between ground with maximum conductivity vs. min. conductivity.

An installer that estimates the ground conductivity will more than likely to use an average number for ground conductivity or estimate the borehole depth/ton using numbers that are prevalent in his region. An oversized loop will be an extra expense but is far better than an undersized loop. An undersized loop will result in low EWT, which results in a low COP and expensive auxiliary heat being used in heating dominated regions. In cooling dominated regions, the EWT will be high, also resulting in a low COP for cooling. In general, the efficiency of the system will be compromised if the system is "short-looped." One variable not considered is the possibility of drilling through an aquifer. Depending on the size and flow rates of water in the aquifer, the heat transfer to/from the loop can be enhanced considerably.

There are some regions of the country where there are underground caverns. Some of these voids can be very large and they could render the borehole useless. Knowledge of below-ground conditions is essential for installing boreholes.

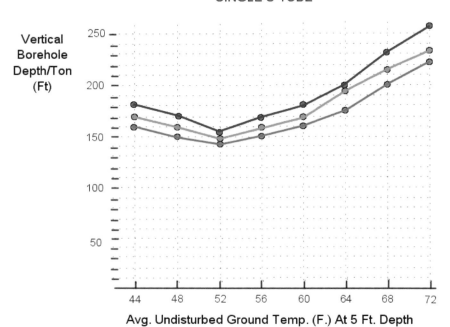

DESIGN OF VERTICAL BOREHOLE LOOP
SINGLE U-TUBE

Vertical
Borehole
Depth/Ton
(Ft)

Avg. Undisturbed Ground Temp. (F.) At 5 Ft. Depth

- 3/4 inch single U-tube (2-pitch)
- 1 inch single U-tube (2-pitch)
- 1 1/4 inch single U-tube (2-pitch)

Note: Pitch is linear length (Ft.) of pipe per foot of borehole.
Ground conductivity=1.2 Btu/hr-ft-degree F.

Figure 7.2.1

The factors which determine the total borehole depth per ton of heating/cooling load needed for a vertical closed loop system are basically the same as for horizontal systems as described in section 6.7.

> **For a Vertical Borehole system, the factors which determine the borehole depth per ton are:**
> **1. The conductivity (k) of the surrounding ground.**
> **2. The conductivity of the grout that surrounds the loop (i.e., the annulus conductivity).**
> **3. The number of "U" tubes placed in each borehole and their diameter. Usually 1 "U" tube per borehole with a diameter of 3/4 inch or 1 inch is installed.**
> **4. The average undisturbed, underground temperature at the location.**

Loops in vertical boreholes are restricted to the simple U-tube configuration. There are three common sizes of vertical HDPE tubing used, which are 3/4 inch, 1 inch and $1\,^1/_4$ inch diameter. To estimate the total depth needed for boreholes in a vertical, closed loop system, the graph displayed in Figure 7.2.1 can be used. Depending on the HDPE pipe diameter, select one of the three graphs shown. Using the average ground temperature at the borehole location (which can be determined from *Appendix A*), locate the corresponding Vertical Borehole Depth-per-Ton on the vertical axis. The three graphs assume a ground conductivity of 1.2 Btu/hr-ft-degree F., which is an average value. Multiply the heat pump's capacity (in tons) by the number just obtained giving the total borehole depth needed. The number of boreholes needed can vary.

In general, the upper limit on borehole depth for residential installations is about 400-450 feet but usually one borehole per ton is drilled giving borehole depths from 145 feet to 230 feet. This results in multiple boreholes connected in parallel and lower water pumping costs. As with circuits in horizontal ground loops, the designer must consider the water flow rate in each circuit necessary for turbulent flow. See section 6.8 *Turbulent Flow and Reynolds Number*.

Because boreholes are deep compared to horizontal loops, the surrounding ground conductivity is higher due mainly to greater compaction of the earth. The graphs of Figure 7.2.1 assumes a ground conductivity of 1.2 Btu/hr-ft-degree F. If a more accurate ground conductivity is known, Table 7.2.1 below can be used to obtain a multiplier factor to be used to adjust the borehole depth/ton obtained from Figure 7.2.1.

Table 7.2.1   BOREHOLE DEPTH/TON ADJUSTMENT FOR GROUND CONDUCTIVITY

Ground conductivity	0.8	1.0	1.2	1.4	1.6	1.8	2.0
Ground Multiplier	1.23	1.10	1.0	.93	.87	.83	.79

Ground conductivity is in Btu/hr-ft-degree F.

The third factor which affects vertical borehole depth per ton is the conductivity of the grout that surrounds the loops within the borehole. This is called **annulus conductivity** and is variable based on the type of thermal grout used.

To take this factor into account, the following table can be used to adjust the vertical borehole depth/ton obtained from Figure 7.2.1 after it is adjusted for ground conductivity using Table

7.2.1. Locate the thermal conductivity of the grout used in the first row of Table 7.2.2. Using the corresponding multiplier factor in the second row, multiply the adjusted result from the graph in Figure 7.2.1 by this factor, giving the adjusted vertical borehole depth/ton based on both ground conductivity and annulus conductivity.

Table 7.2.2 BOREHOLE DEPTH/TON ADJUSTMENT FOR ANNULUS CONDUCTIVITY

Annulus conductivity	0.4	0.6	0.8	1.0	1.2	1.4	1.6
Annulus Multiplier	1.2	1.08	1.01	1.0	.98	.93	.91

Annulus conductivity is in Btu/hr-ft-degree F.

Figure 7.3.1

Figure 7.3.2A

Vertical Borehole Systems

Figure 7.3.2B

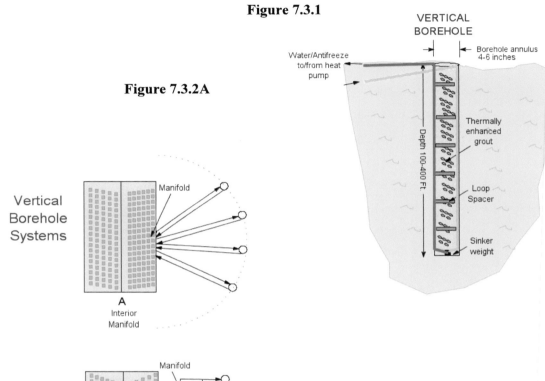

VERTICAL BOREHOLE

Water/Antifreeze to/from heat pump

Borehole annulus 4-6 inches

Depth 100-400 Ft.

Thermally enhanced grout

Loop Spacer

Sinker weight

Manifold

A
Interior Manifold

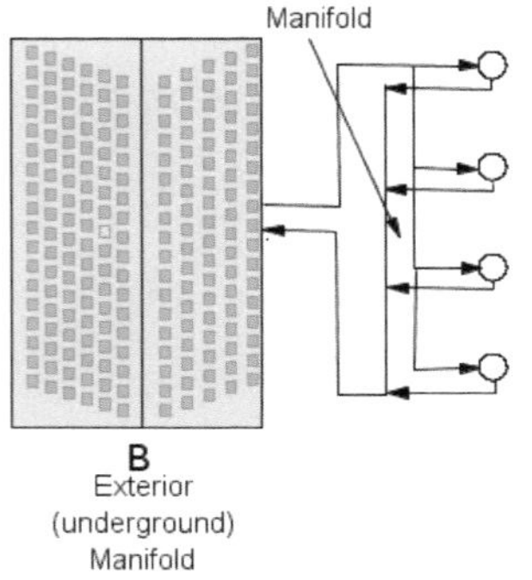

Manifold

B
Exterior (underground) Manifold

7.3 VERTICAL LOOP CONFIGURATION

Unlike the many variations in horizontal closed-loop systems, vertical systems have basically one configuration. Figure 7.3.1 illustrates a vertical borehole with a single, closed loop. The two halves of the loop are joined together with a "U" shaped connector using the fusion welding process. This "U" connector, with tubing attached, has a cast iron weight (known as a **sinker weight**) attached to assist in forcing the loop to the bottom of the borehole. Depth markings on the polypipe, usually at 2 foot intervals, help to verify that the polypipe reaches the bottom of the borehole. This is one measurement the homeowner should monitor while the installation is underway.

When multiple boreholes are needed, it is extremely important that the each borehole loop, or "**circuit**" as they are known, be as close to the same length as possible. This will help to insure that the water flow rate, and therefore the heat transfer, is the same for each borehole, resulting in a balanced system. Sometimes a driller, while drilling a borehole, will encounter a dense obstruction and stop drilling the borehole. He will then go on to drill other boreholes to a greater depth. If he uses boreholes with different depths, using the same size polypipe in each borehole, the system will be unbalanced. The homeowner should address this issue prior to signing a contract for the work, specifying that all boreholes be the same depth.

Ideally, the boreholes should be drilled so that each borehole circuit including the **headers** (the polypipe that extends from the manifold to the heat pump) are the same length as shown in Figure 7.3.2. Figure 7.3.2A illustrates an indoor manifold and Figure 7.3.2 B illustrates an underground manifold loop structure. Ideally, the boreholes should be at least 15 feet apart, preferably 20 feet apart.

> For vertical, closed loop systems, the manifold (the point at which several ground loops converge into a single pair of larger pipes) should preferably be located within the residence. This makes effortless monitoring of temperature, pressure and flow measurements in each loop circuit possible and facilitates troubleshooting. If the distance from the boreholes to the residence is great, an underground outdoor manifold close to the boreholes should be used. If this is the case, a vault made of steel and concrete should be used to house the manifold.

The advice above applies to both horizontal and vertical loops. However, more caution must be used with vertical loops. If an underground manifold is used, the chances of debris (e.g., pebbles) inadvertently entering the loop during installation and becoming lodged at the bottom of the loop are increased. If this happens, it may not be possible to purge the loop of the debris, making the borehole useless. Experienced loop field contractors will cover the ends of the loop pipe to prevent debris and small animals from entering the loop during installation.

7.4 GROUTING VERTICAL LOOPS

After the polypipe, along with a third "**tremie**" grout pipe, is inserted in the borehole, there is air space between the pipe and the surrounding borehole as well as between the two sections of the pipe. Pockets of air are one of the best thermal insulators and to eliminate this insulation, thermal grout is needed. The tremie pipe is used to fill the borehole with grout as it is slowly withdrawn from the borehole. The application of the thermal grout, usually bentonite or preferably a mixture of bentonite and fine-grained sand, should be applied as soon as possible. Any delay, which might result in a collapse of the borehole, would interfere with the proper grouting needed for required thermal transfer. Bentonite grout is supplied in bags, similar to concrete, and must be mixed with water.

> **The borehole grout must be applied from the bottom of the borehole to the top of the borehole using a HDPE tremie pipe, usually 1 inch diameter. The homeowner should observe this process and note the number of bags of grout used in the process and also whether sand is mixed with the grout, which increases its conductivity. Water is added to the mixture to form a slurry. The loop contractor should provide a rough estimate of the amount of grout needed, in the contract.**

It should be noted that there is something that is counterintuitive about adding a thermally conductive grout between the supply and return loops in the borehole. The thermal grout will add to the thermal "short circuiting" between the supply and return lengths of the pipe but it is unavoidable. Spacing brackets (known as **GeoClips**), which are normally spaced about 10 feet apart, have been used to keep the pipe lengths as far apart as possible but some contractors have found them to be difficult to use. The GeoClips do assist in centering the tremie pipe within the borehole and the homeowner should request that they be used.

As mentioned in the horizontal loop chapter, parallel configuration of loops is preferred to a series arrangement when either one will suffice. This applies to vertical loop systems as well. For closed, vertical, ground loop systems, parallel connected loops rather than a long, single circuit with multiple boreholes connected in series should be used to prevent high water pumping costs.

7.5 FLUSHING AND PURGING

Among the final steps in the loop installation is the flushing of the loop with clean water. A high pressure pump, usually at least 2 horsepower, a component of a **purge cart**, is used to make sure no debris is left in the loop. This is usually done with connections at the flow center and purging of air is usually done by reversing the direction of water flow in the loops a few times.

With the water still in the loop, a static pressure test is then made, often at around 100 psi, to insure there are no leaks. After the loops are purged and pressure tested, anti-freeze is added. This is one of the most important steps needed to insure that the loops will not be damaged if the water temperature falls below freezing temperature.

Antifreeze Recommended For Vertical Loops

Loop Config.	Ft-pipe/Ft-trench	% of volume for ground temp. 60-63 F.	% of volume for ground temp. 52-59 F.	% of volume for ground temp 44-51 F.
3/4 " (single pipe)	2	0	10	20
1 1/4" (single pipe)	2	0	10	20

7.6 MISCELLANEOUS

The drilling of boreholes often results in damage to the homeowner's property. The heavy drilling rigs often leave gouged-out and depressed areas that they move over. Also, the excavated material can result in a muddy mound. The homeowner should address these issues early and have the contractual agreement specify the clean-up responsibilities of the loop contractor or general contractor (i.e., the installer). Sometimes underground pipes that were not anticipated are discovered during the excavation process. The homeowner should makes sure the contract spells out the contractor's responsibility for any accidental damage to these pipes and any other property.

When there is a big disparity between heating and cooling loads, which is common in the far north or far south, there is a potential problem. In these areas, the long-term ground temperatures in the loop field may increase (in the south) and decrease (in the north). This is more likely to occur if the loop system is undersized. Therefore, in these areas it is better to be generous when designing the borehole system, especially the separation of boreholes, even though there may be an increase in cost. Of course, if there is subsurface water flow, the long-term effect would be mitigated. As suggested, separation of boreholes by about 20 feet should eliminate the possibility of long-term thermal depletion of the ground around the loops if the correct borehole depth/ton is used.

If there should be a delay between the time the loops are inserted in the borehole(s) and the time when the grout is inserted, which should be avoided, the loops should be filled with water and pressurized to prevent being deformed (i.e., compressed) if some part of the borehole collapses. The homeowner should make sure the installer has the grouting equipment on-site when the drilling begins.

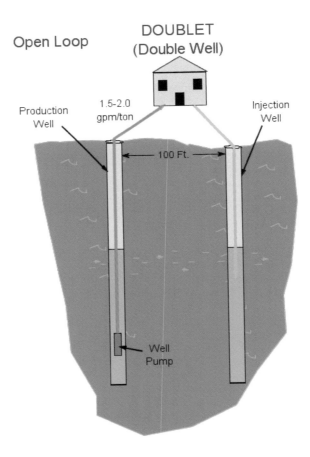

Figure 8.1.1

CHAPTER 8. OPEN LOOP SYSTEMS

As the name implies, open loop systems do not recirculate a fixed quantity of water within an enclosed loop. They circulate water, without any antifreeze, obtained from a body of water, such as a pond, river or, more often, an underground source of water. Because the working fluid does not recirculate within the system, its temperature remains fairly constant. The result is a more efficient system requiring a lower rate of water flow. The heat exchanger used for open loops is usually the cupro-nickel type which is more resistant to dissolved impurities that might be in the well water. Some geo-system installers claim that this type of heat exchanger is only needed if salt water might pass through the heat exchanger but it would be prudent to install this type of heat exchanger. In general, open loop systems take a few different forms.

8.1 GROUND WATER WELLS..... THE DOUBLET

Figure 8.1.1 illustrates the **Doublet** well configuration. This system can only be used where a robust aquifer exists below the proposed location. Two wells that extend deep into the aquifer are drilled. One well is dedicated to the extraction of the working fluid and must have a submerged water pump lowered into it. This well is called the "**production well.**"

The alternate well, known as the "**injection well**", is the place where the working fluid is returned to the same aquifer. The two wells should be as far apart as is practical to insure that no thermal "**short-circuiting**" occurs between the two wells. At least 100 feet of separation should be planned. The injection well should be "**down-gradient**" of the production well. This insures that the injected water will not re-circulate back into the production well.

Not having to re-circulate the same mass of water through the heat pump, as a closed loop system does, the open loop system uses water that has a temperature close to the undisturbed underground temperature. This results in a higher efficiency than closed loop systems. Fluctuations in the EWT (Entering Water Temperature) will have much narrower swings in temperature. The result is a lower water flow rate is required, typically 1.5 to 2 gpm per ton of heating/cooling load, compared to closed loop systems which have a 2.25 to 3 gpm/ton flow rate. The need for deep well boring is usually avoided and therefore, the installation costs are correspondingly lower.

There are, however, disadvantages to open loop systems, including the Doublet, which offset some of the reduced installation cost advantage. The aquifer water often contains dissolved minerals that can create maintenance problems for the heat pump's water-to-refrigerant, coaxial heat exchanger. Dissolved minerals, including calcium carbonate and iron oxides in particular can cause scaling within the heat exchanger requiring more frequent cleaning and shorten the equipment life. Other small debris within the aquifer can also cause maintenance problems. It is important to have the well water analyzed for acidity and mineral content before making the decision to install this type of heat pump system.

Local governmental environmental protection agencies may have oversight in the installation and the ongoing use of groundwater systems. This may require that a permit and inspection be obtained. Probably one of the major concerns of this type of system is the longevity of the aquifer. In an area where there is major development, of both residences and especially nearby industrial construction, the future of the aquifer may be uncertain.

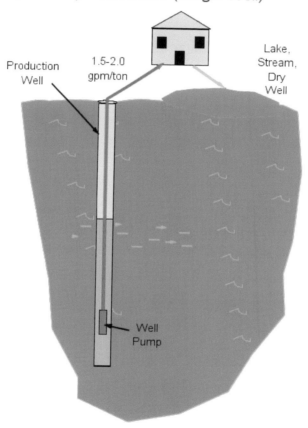

Open Loop   SINGLET (Single Well)

Production Well

1.5-2.0 gpm/ton

Lake, Stream, Dry Well

Well Pump

Figure 8.2.1

8.2 GROUND WATER WELLS.....THE SINGLET

The **Singlet**, or single well groundwater system, uses the production well of the doublet system for obtaining water from the aquifer but eliminates the injection well. Water that passes through the heat pump is dumped into a nearby body of water such as a lake or stream and sometimes onto the ground surface. This is why this configuration is often referred to as "**pump and dump.**" Figure 8.2.1 illustrates this structure. Yet, this is often the most frequent installation of the two types. The lower cost of a single well coupled with the fact that many wells are already in existence to supply potable water makes this a low-cost entry into geothermal heating/cooling as long as the water flow rate is sufficient to provide for both potable water and the heat pump.

There are potential problems with this configuration, mainly the result of local and state environmental regulations. The concern is that if water is dumped on the ground, it may absorb fertilizers, vegetation destroying chemicals, farm and other noxious substances that would eventually find their way into the aquifer. There is also a concern when water is removed from the aquifer and not directly returned to it. If many users, both residential and commercial, pump and dump water, the aquifer could experience wide swings in the level of the water. Therefore, this is not the best heat source/sink for a residential geothermal system.

The well must have an adequate flow rate (usually 1.5 to 2 gpm per ton of heating/cooling load) in order be used for a heat pump in addition to the flow rate needed for other usage. In regions where the ground temperatures are skewed from average values, the flow rate needed would be at the high end of the range. Obviously, all of the problems of heat exchanger scaling and fouling that apply to the doublet also apply to the singlet. The outflow from the singlet must be protected from freezing, which would disable the system. Insulation and pipe burial are usually required.

8.3 OTHER OPEN LOOP SYSTEMS

The **Standing Column Well (SCW)** is a hybrid of open/closed loop systems and is described in the next chapter. An open loop system that receives and rejects water from a surface water supply such as a lake or pond is possible. However, it is not recommended because of the strong possibility of damage to the heat pump's heat exchanger due to debris contained in the water source.

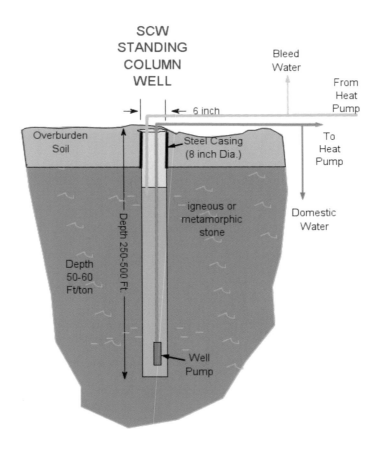

Figure 9.1.1

CHAPTER 9. THE STANDING COLUMN WELL (SCW)

9.1 A HYBRID SYSTEM

The **Standing Column Well (SCW)** is actually a hybrid system that has characteristics of both open loop and closed loop systems. A deep well usually over 200 feet in depth, 6 inches in diameter, is drilled into porous bedrock allowing subsurface ground water to seep into the well. This essentially forms a "container" in the shape of a cylinder from which water can be pumped from , and sent to, a heat pump for both heating and cooling purposes and then returned to the same well. Figure 9.1.1 illustrates the basic construction of a SCW.

The SCW is most common in the Northeast USA, generally from New York and states to its north although there are SCWs south of New England in Virginia and the Carolinas. The geology in these regions is characterized by thick, subsurface, igneous or metamorphic rock formation suitable for this type of well. Most existing SCWs are used in heating dominated regions. The top section of the well is protected with an 8 inch diameter steel casing from the surface to the entry point in the bedrock. This is necessary because the material above the bedrock consists of soft collapsible material which would, if the casing was not there, fall into the well. The casing also prevents contamination of the well from surface water which contains various pollutants.

A pump is lowered to a position near the bottom of the well and has to be of sufficient power to pump water to the heat pump at a rate of about 3 gpm per ton of heat pump capacity. After being used by the heat pump, the water is reinjected to the SCW near the top of the well but below the surface level of the water in the well, which is at the level of the water table. How deep does the well have to be? In general, a minimum depth of 50 to 60 feet of borehole depth per ton of heating capacity is needed.

Standing Column wells more than 800 feet in depth, primarily commercial installations, use a **Porter Shroud**. This is a PVC pipe about 4 inches in diameter that is inserted into the borehole and extends to the bottom of the borehole. Holes are drilled into the bottom of this dip tube to allow the warmest water to enter at the bottom and be drawn up within the inner dip tube. The pump is positioned near the top, and inside of the Porter Shroud, thereby allowing a smaller pump with a shorter electrical cable to be used. The water return line from the heat pump is inserted between the outer surface of the dip tube and the inner surface of the well borehole below the surface of the water in the well.

9.2 BLEED FLOW

Theoretically, the SCW is a column of a fixed amount of water and if too much heat is withdrawn from the well, the well might not be able to supply sufficient heat if used continuously during the coldest periods. While this would be true if the well was in a fixed container, the surrounding bedrock is porous and capable of replacing water that is withdrawn from the well.

A process called "**bleeding**" is used to prevent the water in the SCW from becoming too cold in the winter and too hot in the summer. By bleeding , or not returning a portion of the water to the well, the water in the surrounding bedrock replaces the water removed in a process called **advection**. Advection does not come into play only during bleed cycles, the normal pumping of water from the bottom of the borehole and through the heat pump causes a circulation of water into and out of the nearby porous wall of the borehole. Various amounts of water can be automatically bled from the SCW to prevent water temperature from nearing the freezing point and being drawn into, and damaging, the heat pump's heat exchanger. Sometimes the SCW is also used to provide domestic potable water usage; a natural from of bleeding. By increasing the borehole depth per ton from the average 50-60 feet to higher figures, the necessary bleed rate can be reduced. This is true for both heating dominant usage as well as cooling dominant applications.

Water that is bled from the system can be disposed of in nearby bodies of water. Local ordinances, concerning the extraction and disposition of ground water must be evaluated before a SCW is considered.

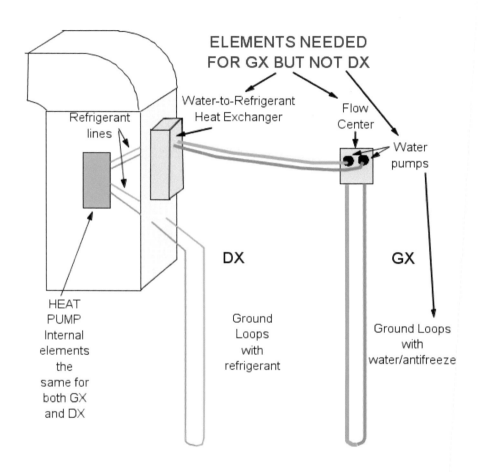

ELEMENTS NEEDED
FOR GX BUT NOT DX

Water-to-Refrigerant
Heat Exchanger

Flow
Center

Refrigerant
lines

Water
pumps

DX

GX

HEAT
PUMP
Internal
elements
the
same for
both GX
and DX

Ground
Loops
with
refrigerant

Ground Loops
with
water/antifreeze

Figure 10.1.1 Comparison of GX to DX System

CHAPTER 10. (DX) DIRECT EXCHANGE SYSTEM

10.1 NO WATER NEEDED!

Residential geo-systems are broadly categorized as either water-based (open or closed loop) or refrigerant-based (closed loop), depending on which working fluid is used in the ground loop to transfer thermal energy. Up to this point, only water-based systems have been described. This chapter deals with the refrigerant-based system, commonly known as **DX** (**D**irect-e**X**change).

DX systems are much less complex than water-based systems. Figure 10.1.1 illustrates the basic components of a DX system. As shown in the drawing, an entire heat transfer interface which is part of water-based systems is unnecessary in a DX system. The components that are missing from DX systems are:

1. The HDPE water-based loops.
2. The tube-in-tube, coaxial, water-to-refrigerant heat exchanger.
3. Water and antifreeze.
4. The Water pump(s) and flow center.
5. Installation functions including flushing and static pressure testing of water loops.
6. Temperature and pressure gauges to monitor loop water conditions.

The elimination of the above from DX systems are a few of the reasons why this type of system is 20-25% more efficient than comparable GX systems and also cost less to install. By eliminating the water pump(s), there is a reduction in electrical usage.

The DX system closely parallels the household refrigerator described in *Chapter 4*. Recall that the residential refrigerator transfers heat from within the envelope of the refrigerator to the condenser coils usually located at the bottom or rear of the refrigerator and from there into the room where the refrigerator is located. The operation of a DX system works in the same way. In the heating mode, a DX system consists of the evaporator (i.e., the heat absorber) which is soft copper tubing filled with refrigerant buried below ground and the condenser (i.e., the heat emitter) is an indoor heat exchanger which can transfer heat from the refrigerant coil to an interior air-based or water-based sub-system. Unlike a refrigerator, the DX system can reverse the flow of refrigerant with a **reversing valve**, switching from a heating to a cooling mode so that the indoor heat exchanger becomes the evaporator, absorbing indoor heat and transferring that heat to the subsurface copper loops, which reverse their role and become the condenser.

Ground loops for DX systems are smaller, for the same tonnage, than water-based systems for several reasons. Copper tubing is more efficient than HDPE pipe for heat transmission. At a heat transmission rate of 19 BTU per sq. ft per hour per degree F. per inch of pipe wall thickness, compared to 2.7 for HDPE, copper is close to 6 times more efficient in heat transmission. However, the biggest impediment to heat transfer is the conductivity of the earth surrounding the tubing. The higher rate of heat transfer with refrigerants occurs because of a phase change (i.e., from a liquid to vapor, or vice versa), resulting in much higher temperature differentials (between the ground and refrigerant fluid in the loops) compared to water flowing in HDPE ground loops. This higher temperature differential results in higher efficiency for DX loops and requires shorter lengths of tubing. This reduces the loop field installation costs, for both vertical and horizontal DX installations, compared to water-based systems. Even the drilling rigs needed for vertical boring are smaller; an eight foot rig for DX in comparison to a 22 foot rig for water-base. DX residential systems are currently restricted to heat pump sizes in the 2 to 6 ton range. However, it must be pointed out that the separation of horizontal loops and vertical boreholes must be greater than their water-based counterparts due to the greater efficiency of heat extraction/rejection described above. Therefore, even though the loop size for DX is smaller than for GX (per ton) the total loop field area may be larger.

> **DX systems use a much smaller loop size compared to GX systems:**
> **Horizontal DX uses about 350 Ft./ton vs. GX horizontal loop use of about 600-1000 Ft./ton and even more for Slinky-type loops. Vertical DX uses about 100-130 Ft. of borehole/ton vs. GX uses about 150-220 Ft. of borehole/ton.**

DX systems, based on the heat transfer comparison described above, have a basic advantage over water- based (GX) systems in regions with extreme (hot or cold) temperatures. The efficiency (i.e., the COP) of water-based closed loop systems becomes much lower compared to DX systems when there are extremes in temperature.

Even though the first DX geothermal heat pump system was built in the late 1940s by Robert Webber, water-based/ground loop geo-systems (GX) far exceed the number of DX systems installed today. I believe this imbalance will change. It is my opinion that electrical rates will rise appreciably in the near future due to a worldwide environmental-conscious movement and as noted, DX systems , if properly installed, require less electrical usage per ton of heating/cooling than GX systems.

In all DX systems the ground loops must be located as close to the residence as possible. The compressor cannot be placed at great distances from the ground loops due to the excessive amount of refrigerant that would be needed, resulting in larger compressors. Many DX systems will have the **manifold** (i.e., the connection of all loop circuits into a single pair of pipes) located underground near the ground loops but indoor manifolds are used when the loops/boreholes are very close to the residence. In fact, some DX systems have each ground loop circuit directly connected to the heat pump. In other words, both vapor and liquid lines are independently, directly connected to the heat pump allowing the system to manage each loop based on variable load conditions. This allows, for example, fewer loops to be used in cooling mode, mitigating the "short-cycling" problem. **Nordic**, one major DX heat pump manufacturer, manufactures this type of heat pump. This heat pump even has the operation of the soaker hose integrated with the heat pump.

Less flexible are the outdoor, underground manifolds which merge multiple ground loops into a pair of headers. They reduce the refrigerant loop considerably, requiring a smaller amount of refrigerant as well as limiting the size of the compressor. This setup requires that the copper loops be connected to copper manifolds using a brazing operation that requires a highly skilled installer. Any possibility of refrigerant loop leakage is more likely to occur at the brazed joints than anywhere else. The installer must be skilled in testing the loops for leaks, adding the proper amount of refrigerant, correctly pressurizing the loops, connecting the desuperheater to the domestic hot water tank(s) and testing the system. The copper refrigerant loops should be pressurized to about 400psi with nitrogen gas for an 8 hour period to insure there are no leaks.

Horizontal DX ground loop systems require less pipe length per ton than comparable GX systems. However, they usually require a larger ground surface area because they must be spaced at a much greater separation. Trench width is generally 4 feet compared to the 3 foot width commonly used for GX systems. Vertical DX boreholes also require a larger surface area than comparable GX systems. DX boreholes must be separated by about 20 feet to avoid **thermal interference** between the borehole loops that would result in excessive thermal depletion of the surrounding earth.

Just about all DX loops use parallel circuits, with 1 ton of heating load capacity per circuit. The first 12 feet of the tubing outside the residence, both liquid and vapor lines, must be insulated to prevent freezing of the ground near and under the home's foundation. This will prevent damage to the home from freezing and thawing of the ground below the foundation. Also, all interior refrigerant lines must be insulated to prevent condensation. The heat pump should be located as close to the central point of the home in order to minimize duct work and produce a balanced system.

The warranty on the copper ground loops often extend to 20-50 years depending on the heat pump manufacturer. The alkalinity of the soil should be tested before installation. If the acidity of the soil is high (pH of 5.5 or below) a **sacrificial anode** should be installed to prevent deterioration of the copper loop. DX systems, like their GX counterpart, can also supply domestic hot water using a desuperheater, also known as a **Hot Water Generator (HWG)**.

EarthLinked Technologies, the most well known supplier of DX systems, recommends that electrical supplemental heat (i.e., heat strips) with a rating of 20% of design heating load be a required component of the system. This is understandable because DX systems can withdraw large amounts of thermal energy from the ground in a very short time period. Having a sizeable supplementary heat source to permit temporary thermal recharging of the near-loop ground is desirable under extremely cold conditions. Consequently, generous separation of DX loops is the rule rather than the exception. Thermostat setbacks can be problematic for both water-based and DX geo-systems because the heat pump must "work overtime" to regain the higher setpoint temperature. This is more of a problem for DX systems because the possibility of freezing the ground increases dramatically and this could damage the copper pipes as well as the home's foundation. Most DX systems are considered 2- stage systems; a single stage heat pump with second stage auxiliary heat strips. Often, the system is designed so that the auxiliary strips will automatically activate after the heat pump runs continuously for about 30 minutes.

Residential Geothermal systems are not Do-It-Yourself (**DIY**) projects, especially DX systems. Handling of large amount of refrigerants, that may be hot and under high pressure, is a safety concern. The size of the heat pump and design of loop field must be coordinated by the same, highly experienced, personnel resulting in a minimum of outside subcontractors. Also, the system's warranty is dependent upon the installer being authorized and trained by the heat pump manufacturer.

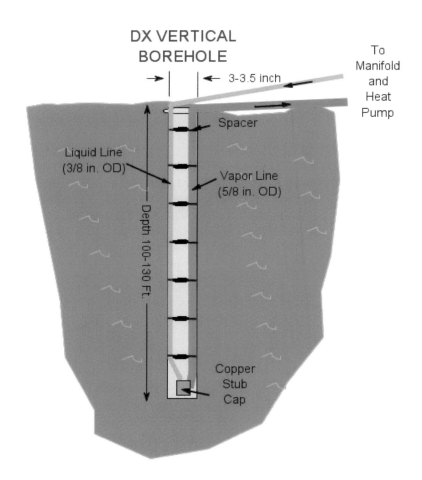

Figure 10.2.1

10.2 VERTICAL DX SYSTEMS

Vertical boreholes for DX systems are not as deep as those for comparable water-based, ground loop geo-systems. On average, a borehole depth of 100 to 120 feet per ton of heating/cooling capacity is required. If the boreholes are installed in regions of temperature extremes, either hot or cold, the borehole depth/ton should be at least 120-135 feet/ton. Usually one borehole per ton of heating/cooling load is excavated, requiring 200 to 240 feet of copper tubing per ton. There are some differences compared to water-based installations. Since the loop placed in the borehole will contain refrigerant that is in both a liquid and vapor state, the two halves of the loop will have different diameters. The half containing mostly liquid refrigerant will be the smaller diameter tubing, usually $^3/_8$ inch OD (Outer Diameter) and the vapor half usually $^5/_8$ inch (OD). While HDPE tubes are connected at the bottom of the borehole with a "U" shaped connector, copper tubes use a **copper stub cap**, generally $^7/_8$ inch by 1 inch, to join the two halves of different sized copper tubes together, by brazing. Figure 10.2.1 illustrates this construction. Spacers to separate and hold the two lengths of copper tubing apart are necessary to prevent thermal "short-circuiting." With water-based pipes this is less important and often not used, but with high temperature differentials using copper tubing, spacers are mandatory. The spacers are placed about 5 feet apart.

A borehole diameter from 3 to 3 ½ inches is commonly used for DX systems. After the copper loop is placed in the borehole, a grout fill material is added to insure good thermal contact between the tubing and surrounding borehole wall. Unlike the grout used in closed water-based loops, DX systems use a plasticsized grout that must remain flexible due to the wider extremes in the loop temperature. If the borehole is drilled in an area with abundant ground water, pea gravel is often used to fill the borehole up to the ground water level. This provides space for the ground water to circulate around the tubing and enhances thermal transfer. Above the ground water level, the expandable thermal grout is used to provide the thermal conductivity with the surrounding ground as well as keeping surface ground water from polluting any subsurface aquifer.

When multiple boreholes are needed, generally with each borehole having one ton of heating capacity, their spacing is important. A minimum of 20 feet separation between all adjacent boreholes is the rule for vertical boreholes in order to prevent thermal interference, depletion of the ground and reduce the possibility of freezing or buckling of the tubing when in heating mode. However, when the boreholes are drilled diagonally, the position of the boreholes at the surface can be closer than 20 feet because the boreholes spread apart with depth to form a cone-shape configuration. In order to keep the amount of refrigerant to a minimum, the boreholes should be placed as close as possible to the tubing entry point in the residence.

Insulation of the copper headers (i.e., the tubing from the manifold, if it is outdoors, to the interior compressor of the heat pump) is required. At minimum, the 12 foot length of outdoor tubing closest to the residence should be insulated to prevent freezing of the ground at the foundation. Generally, **Armaflex** insulation is used.

DX systems, especially those with horizontal loops or diagonal boreholes, usually have a soaker hose embedded in the ground above the loops to maintain efficiency when the system is in cooling mode. The high, copper tubing temperatures can dry out the surrounding soil, diminishing the earth's thermal conductivity and reducing the system's COP.

Earth is not a perfect heat sink/heat source that can absorb or supply heat with no effect on its long-term temperature. In some geo-systems, especially large commercial ones, the earth surrounding the loops will gradually increase in temperature over a period of years. Ground temperature increases of 6 degrees F. over a 10 year period have been recorded at some of these larger installations. This is less likely to happen with smaller residential systems, especially if borehole separation guidelines , as described above, are followed.

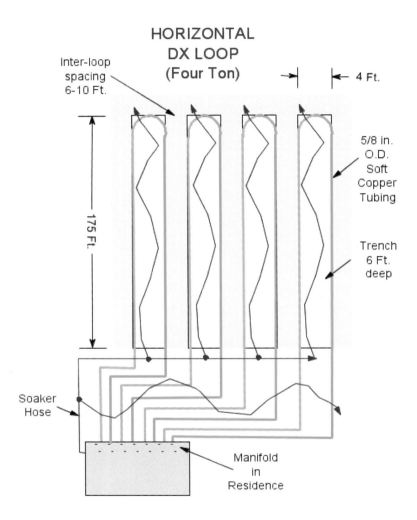

Figure 10.3.1

10.3 HORIZONTAL DX SYSTEMS

The horizontal DX system is installed in the same fashion as a straight one-loop-per-trench (also known as a 2-pipe) GX water-based system. There are no horizontal "Slinky" DX loop systems. In general, a minimum of about 1750 square feet per ton of land area is needed for a horizontal DX system primarily due to the wide loop separation required. Figure 10.3.1 illustrates the basic loop structure for a 4 ton system; one trench per ton. As with vertical DX systems, the manifold can be located within the residence's utility room and sometimes in the heat pump itself. Only certain heat pumps provide the latter integrated manifold construction. If the trenches are near the residence, the heat pump integrated manifold setup is ideal if the heat pump selected has this capability. Otherwise, the manifolds can be located within the basement or placed in an outdoor, underground pit, covered with a header box, as close to the trenches as possible. The two pipe headers then transport the liquid/vapor refrigerant to the heat pump. The entire ground loop tubing is usually ½ inch diameter (OD). If the manifold is integrated into the heat pump unit, the liquid line must be reduced to $^3/_8$ inch diameter as it passes through the basement wall.

Trenches are normally 4 feet in width, which is wider than the average 3 feet used for GX systems due to the possibility of thermal interference, as previously described. The separation of trenches is dependent on the type of subsurface material (i.e., soil, sand, clay etc.) and its moisture content. In general, 6 to 10 feet of separation between adjacent trenches is recommended; the wider the better. DX loops are most effective in moist sandy soils. It has been suggested that horizontal DX loops should be slightly inclined so that the loop section furthest away from the residence is higher than the loop entering the residence. The logic behind this is that gravity will assist the return of liquid refrigerant to the compressor. A soaker hose, as illustrated in Figure 10.3.1, is buried below the frost line above the copper loops and is used to enhance thermal conductivity during extremely long hot dry spells.

10.4 COPPER LOOP CORROSION

One aspect of DX systems has discouraged potential customers; the possibility of deterioration and leaking of a copper refrigerant line beneath the ground understandably concerns people. In reality, this should not be a major concern. Today, underground copper pipes for potable water for residences are standard and are expected to last 50 years or more. Although copper pipe or tubing used in DX systems is not as thick as that used for residential water systems because they must have more flexibility, they will last just as long if certain precautions are taken. First, the pH (i.e., the acidity) of the ground in which the copper loops will be placed must be tested. The pH should be between 5.5 and 10. Needless to say, areas where there are potential ground contaminants such as farm runoff or manufacturing waste, should be carefully evaluated. Trees should not be planted near the trenches in order to avoid possible damage from roots.

Additionally, there are some steps that can be taken to reduce the possibility of copper pipe corrosion. EarthLinked Technologies, one of the major manufacturers of DX systems, developed a **Cathode Protection System (CPS)** which uses a small electric rectifier to supply a low level, direct current to the underground loop. This steady current discourages the oxidation of copper, thereby preventing leaks. As mentioned previously, the most likely place where loops could leak would be in the brazed joints at the manifolds. If the manifolds are located in the home's interior, the possibility of this leakage is diminished and detection enhanced.

Damage to a DX loop is more likely to occur if the loop is undersized. DX loops extract heat from the ground at a rapid rate and an undersized loop could cause freezing and thawing of the ground surrounding the loop. **The possibility of damage from the freezing/thawing is the biggest threat to the copper loop.**

10.5 POTENTIAL PROBLEMS

The DX system is a fully refrigerant system as opposed to a water-source geo-system. Therefore, most problems will be identified by abnormal refrigerant pressure in various parts of the system. There is a high pressure and a low pressure part of the system. The high pressure side begins at the output line of the compressor and extends to the **TXV** (Thermostatic eXpansion Valve, a refrigerant metering device), which is a used to lower the refrigerant temperature and pressure. The TXV is the equivalent of the capillary tube in the refrigerator. The low pressure side extends from the TXV through the loop field, the reversing valve to the input of the compressor. The heat pump control unit will shut down the heat pump under two conditions:

The **low pressure side** refrigerant pressure drops below 20 psi. This would usually indicate:
    —Low refrigerant charge, or,
    _Leak in the ground loop
The **high pressure side** refrigerant pressure is too high. This would usually indicate:
    _ Either the air filter and/or finned-tube heat exchanger is dirty, or,
    _ Air blower fan belt is defective

Refrigerant pressure on the low pressure side is called the **suction pressure** and its range should be near 54-58 psi. Refrigerant pressure on the high pressure side is called the

discharge pressure and its range should be near 225-275 psi. A lockout condition arises when the suction or discharge pressures fall out of their acceptable range. The unit can be reactivated by turning the thermostat to off, then on, but the unit needs immediate service from the installer if this lockout repeats. The homeowner should rely on the auxiliary heat strips until the unit is repaired. As with GX systems, the advice given repeatedly in this book must be repeated again:

The size of the ground loop is critical to the success of any geo-system. Installing a loop larger than what is considered average should be a goal of the homeowner who is installing a residential geothermal system.

CHAPTER 11. THE MANUAL-J

11.1 WHAT IS A MANUAL-J?

The word "**Manual-J**" is one of the most common words used in residential, geothermal system discussions. This term represents an analysis of a residence to determine the heating/cooling load and therefore, the size of the heat pump(s) and the loop field needed to adequately provide heating and cooling. In the past, the Manual-J calculations were done without the aid of computers. Today, geo-system designers/contractors use computer programs to facilitate the calculation. Any bidder who does not verify that he has used one of these software programs should be eliminated from contention. The bidder might not want to immediately provide the homeowner with a copy of the Manual-J report. This is understandable because if he doesn't win the contract, he will have expended a good deal of time without being compensated. He is obligated, of course, to provide the design heating and cooling loads when making the bid. The homeowner could ask the bidder for a copy of the report at the time the bid is made and if denied, ask to purchase the report with the understanding that the cost of the Manual-J would be deducted from the installation price if the bid was accepted. It would not be unreasonable to pay $100-$200 for a Manual-J report.

In order to produce the Manual-J, the bidder must obtain extensive information about the residence. Sizes of all rooms, windows and their U-values, doors, insulation installed and the R-value, etc. are needed. It would facilitate the process if the homeowner gathered as much of this information as possible before meeting with the bidder.

The Manual-J will estimate the heat loss/heat gain of the home. These figures will be in tons, where 1 ton is 12,000 BTUs/hr. The estimate will be, just that, an estimate because there are some facts which are sometimes not known. In older homes, for example, the amount and R-value of insulation in walls may not be known. Sometimes insulation sags at the top of the wall cavities, lessening its effectiveness. Cracks and crevices would cause greater heat and cooling losses on windy days. These conditions might not be accurately taken into account in a Manual-J. A **blower-door test** and follow-up sealing of leaks found should be performed.

The Design Heating and Cooling Load calculated by the Manual-J process does depend on a variable specified by the homeowner. The variable is the desired thermostat settings (i.e., **setpoints**) for heating and cooling. The two Design Loads can vary considerably based on the homeowner's expected comfort levels, therefore the geo-system size and install cost will vary depending on the desired thermostat setting. The following is an example of a Manual- J report. It will give the homeowner an idea of some of the data which must be collected.

Manual-J **PROJECT SUMMARY**
Homeowner's Name: John Doe   Contractor Name: XYZ Co.
Address: 100 Main Street   Address: 10 Smith St.
        Anywhere, USA   Anywhere, USA

DESIGN CONDITIONS

Location: Anywhere, USA   Infiltration:
Elevation: 400 Ft.   Building Tightness: Loose
Latitude: 46 degrees N.   No. of Fireplaces: 2
                            Method Used: Simplified

INDOOR:	Heat	Cool	**OUTDOOR:**	Heat	Cool
Setpoint (F.)			Dry Bulb (F.)	5	88
(Design Temp)	68	75	Wet Bulb (F.)		72
Differential(F.)	63	13	Daily Range		20 (Med)
Moisture			Wind Speed (mph)	19	9
Diff. (Gr/lb)	21	33			

	HEATING Load			**COOLING Load**		
Structure	**Heat transfer per sq-ft (Btuh/ft²)**	**Total Heat transfer rate (Btuh)**	**% of Load**	**Heat transfer per sq-ft (Btuh/ft²)**	**Total Heat transfer rate (Btuh)**	**% of Load**
Ceilings	2	2500	5	1.8	2200	8.1
Doors	18	420	.8	9.5	204	.6
Glazing	26	7900	14.2	32.2	9218	35
Floors	1	1380	3	.2	54	.6
Ventilation		2340	4.8		650	3.9
Ducts		6450	8.7		6100	23
Piping		0	0	0	0	0
Infiltration	8.2	16226	29	1.5	2320	9.6
Walls	5.6	18650	34	2.1	5200	19.2
Misc.	.2	500	.5	0	0	0
Total		56366	100		25946	100

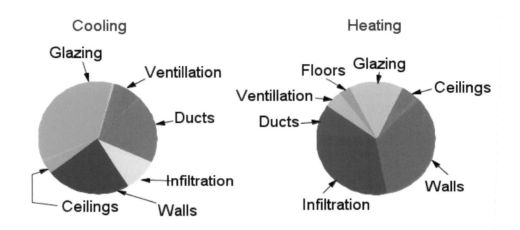

Cooling   Heating

Utility Costs

Fuel Type	Rate	Summer	Winter
Natural Gas	$/CCF	0.75	1.20
#2Fuel Oil	$/gal	1.80	2.50
Propane	$/gal	1.95	2.80
Electric - Geo	$/kWh	0.18	0.18

Operating Costs

System Description	Eff(%) Htg/Clg	Heating Cost	Cooling Cost	Hydronic Cost	Hot Water Cost	Fan	Tot Op $	Mnth $
Heat Pump Model and Loop Config.	3.4/18	$750	$180		$450	$65	1445	121

Note: heating efficiency (COP)/cooling efficiency (EER)

Sample Manual-J
SYSTEM PERFORMANCE BIN DATA

Weather		System Loads		Heat Pump XYZ					AUX.	HW
OAT (F.)	Yrly Hrs	Space Btuh	HW Btuh	Avg Loop Temp	Air Btuh	HW Btuh	Run Time %	Total Kwh	Aux Elect Kwh	HW Elect Kwh
102	1	46100	2326	95	46100	2326	100%	4	0	0
97	14	39264	2326	87	39264	2326	100%	38	0	0
92	61	32428	2326	79	38572	2767	84%	127	0	0
87	189	25592	2326	72	39218	3565	65%	291	0	0
82	345	18756	2326	66	39790	3276	47%	367	0	86
77	545	11920	2326	59	40352	2637	30%	347	0	269
72	790	0	2326	53	0	0	0%	0	0	585
67	823	0	2326	53	0	0	0%	0	0	610
62	753	0	2326	53	0	0	0%	0	0	558
57	757	-1020	2326	55	32127	5241	3%	73	0	521
52	685	-4945	2326	52	31190	5125	16%	320	0	330
47	682	-8870	2326	50	30255	5009	29%	575	0	186
42	758	-12796	2326	47	29320	4893	44%	927	0	46
37	901	-16721	2326	45	29210	4064	57%	1412	0	0
32	766	-20646	2326	42	29103	3279	71%	1453	0	0
27	393	-24572	2326	40	28770	2724	85%	877	0	0
22	170	-28497	2326	38	28497	2326	100%	437	0	0
17	87	-32422	2326	35	32422	2326	100%	257	0	0
12	33	-36347	2326	33	36347	2326	100%	110	0	0
7	9	-40273	2326	33	36848	2326	100%	31	9	0
2	3	-44198	2326	33	36848	2326	100%	10	6	0
	8765							7654	15	3191

BIN(ning) is the process of grouping temperature data into data classes **OAT** Outside Air Temp **HW** Hot Water

Most of the terms used in the Manual-J example should be familiar to the reader. A few that might not be are described below.

In **Design Conditions**, the **Temperature Differential** is the difference between the setpoint and the outdoor Design temperature. For heating mode this is 63 (68 - 5) and for cooling mode this is 13 (88 - 75) in the sample report shown.

The **Outdoor Daily Range** (in temperature) is the average difference between the daily high and low temperatures.

Dry Bulb and **Wet Bulb** temperatures. Dry bulb temperature is the temperature indicated on a regular thermometer that is shielded from radiation and moisture. This is the temperature that you hear on local weather forecasts. Wet bulb temperature is obtained by taking a regular thermometer and covering the bulb with a piece of moist muslin. Movement of air across the bulb will evaporate water from the covered bulb, reducing its temperature. The lower the ambient humidity, the lower the dry bulb temperature will be. At 100% humidity, both thermometers will have the same reading.

Moisture Difference is the difference in the content of indoor vs. outdoor moisture measured in grains/pound.

In **Heating and Cooling Loads**, the contribution of each element in the home toward both load types is detailed. Not shown is the room-by-room breakdown for the loads and the corresponding **Air Volume Flow (AVF)** in cubic feet per minute required for each room.

The **System Performance Bin Data** provides the number of annual hours expected for various outdoor temperatures at the locality of the residence along with the corresponding heating (-) and cooling (+) loads. Performance data for the specific heat pump selected is provided. Estimated usage of electricity for a separate hot water heater, assumed to consume electricity only when the heat pump is inactive, is also provided.

11.2 COST OF GEO-SYSTEMS

One of the biggest problems facing a potential homeowner in deciding whether to install a geo-system is the installation cost. Unlike a conventional heating/cooling system where a fuel, whose BTU heat content is well known, a geo-system is not generating heat but transferring heat to and from a fickle environment, the ground, at a relatively slow rate. This being the case, much more planning and estimating must be performed to install a geo-system of the proper size. Also, geo-systems are relatively new in comparison to conventional systems and therefore, there are a lot fewer HVAC personnel that have the skill and knowledge needed to estimate the size of, and install these systems. This puts a lot of the burden on the homeowner to do his "due diligence" before making the decision to "go Geo."

The installation costs associated with a geo-system can be divided into two categories:
1. Interior equipment and installation costs.
2. Exterior ground loop system and installation costs.

The interior costs can be broken down as follows:

DUCT SYSTEM:
If the existing duct system is large enough, no duct replacement expense is incurred. On new construction or an undersized existing system, the duct system must be installed/replaced. Expect to pay from $6000 to $10000 based on zoning, number of rooms, etc. It is very important to have this done correctly. One of the biggest problems with geo-systems is the installation of a heat pump that is too big for the duct system. This situation will result in a less efficient, troublesome system. It is important to make sure that flex-canvas connections to the supply and return ducts at the heat pump are installed to reduce noise problems. Proper sealing of the ducts to prevent leaks is critical for achieving the COP rating of the heat pump.

HEAT PUMP:
Heat pumps are built by quite a few manufacturers. Some of them are listed in *Appendix C*. Heat Pumps are sized in tons and for the average home a heat pump in the range of 2 to 6 tons is commonly used. Quite often two heat pumps are installed instead of a single very large unit. Two heat pumps can share the same loop field. The per-ton incremental cost for heat pumps is high, sometimes as much as a few thousand dollars. There are other reasons not to install an oversized heat pump, as explained in *Chapter 5*, in addition to the excessive installation cost. The brand of heat pump selected is often dependent upon the installer's relationship to the manufacturer and his experience with a particular line of heat pumps from a single or a few manufacturers. Expect to pay about $2000 dollars per ton for the heat pump itself.

Heat pumps have a compressor that is either single-speed or two-speed. Unless the heat pump is very small, a heat pump with a two-speed compressor should be selected. This will result in lower electrical costs and better dehumidification when the demand on the heat pump is low. It will also reduce the wear and tear on the compressor resulting in less short-cycling and a longer useful life of the compressor. Two-speed compressors work better with zone-controlled systems. These systems allow individual rooms to maintain different temperatures through the use a zone controller and automatic dampers.

HEAT PUMP OPTIONAL EQUIPMENT:
Some heat pump features are built-in at the factory and some are optional, depending on the manufacturer. For example, the desuperheater can be an additional option in a heat pump or it can be factory installed. An integrated unit is recommended. Currently, the 30% tax credit (in the USA) may require the desuperheater (also known as a hot water generator) to be installed. If a desuperheater has to be installed separately, it will probably cost $400-$600. The water-to-refrigerant heat exchanger is either made of copper or cupronickel, the latter being required for open loops and is an added expense.

The geo-system thermostat is different from the commonly used ones found in most homes. It has to control many more functions. This is not a place to try to save a few dollars. The thermostat has to control first, second and third stages of the heat pump. A thermostat that can indicate when these stages are active will provide the homeowner with a valuable tool to monitor the system. For example, if the thermostat has this capability, and it indicates third stage (electric heat strips) are being used when the outdoor temperature is not very cold, this could indicate a problem with the system. It would also result in a higher electric bill than was anticipated.

Some models of heat pumps are equipped with *ECM* variable-speed or dual-speed motors on their air handler fans (blowers). The variable-speed controls for these fans attempt to keep the air moving at a comfortable velocity, minimizing cool drafts and maximizing electrical savings. It also minimizes the noise from the blower running at full speed.

Scroll compressors are another advance in heat pump technology which consists of two spiral-shaped scrolls. While one remains stationary, the other orbits around it, compressing the refrigerant by forcing it into increasingly smaller areas. Compared to typical piston compressors, scroll compressors are quieter and have a longer operating life. Performance data shows that heat pumps with scroll compressors provide 10°–15°F (5.6°–8.3°C) warmer air when in the heating mode, compared to heat pumps using piston compressors.

Most heat pumps use electric resistance heaters (i.e., aux. heating strips) as a backup for extremely cold weather. Alternatively, heat pumps can also be equipped with backup-burners to supplement the heat pump. During extremely cold weather, these burners provide the same function as the aux. heating strips. Backup heat sources increase comfort by avoiding the circulation of relatively cool air during unusually cold weather. Most heat pump manufacturers do not provide this non-electric heat backup capability. It is usually implemented with a separate unit that shares the same ductwork. Fuels used in this configuration include natural gas, fuel oil, propane or even coal and wood. Cost savings for these alternate heat backup sources will depend on the relative cost of electricity vs. these other fuels.

The cost of electricity in your area may have the biggest impact on your decision to install a geo-system vs. a conventional heating and cooling system. Use the table 2.6.2 in *Chapter 2* as a guide to determine whether a geo-system will be cheaper to run than a non-geo system. **Everything depends on the relative cost of different fuels!** This advice is extremely important to readers who live in some northeast USA locations where electric rate are very high. Any use of auxiliary heat strips in these areas will be very expensive. Aside from the possibility of rapid price increases in natural gas, there are a few other circumstances in which higher electric cost might be less onerous. Many localities are starting to offer time-of-day electric rates to encourage usage during off-peak hours. As mentioned in an earlier chapter, a geo-system utilizing a radiant heating system with a large thermal mass could be set up so that the heat pump only runs during the cheaper, off-peak hours. Also, photovoltaic solar systems can offset higher electric costs for geo-systems.

The success of the implementation of a geo-system depends primarily on the choice of system designer/installer. This is due to the fact that the number of highly trained and highly experienced HVAC personnel in this specific field is not high. The homeowner's most challenging task is to find the most experienced designers/installers who are certified and accredited to install a geo-system. The International Ground Source Heat Pump Association (IGSHPA) website can assist in locating experienced personnel:

http://www.igshpa.okstate.edu/directory/directory.asp

Another source is:

http://directory.geoexchange.org

CHAPTER 12. FINAL STEPS

12.1 OBTAINING INSTALLER BIDS

The following flowcharts are meant to guide the homeowner who is considering acquiring a geothermal heating and cooling system. *Flowchart 1* summarizes the initial tasks that a homeowner should concentrate on. Making sure that the home is insulated to the maximum is essential before considering a geo-system. If that is not done, an oversized and expensive heat pump unit will be required. Second, the prospective geo-system owner should learn as much as possible about residential geothermal systems. This book should have impressed upon the reader the extensive knowledge needed to make an intelligent decision as to whether to install such a system and what features and options are available.

It is not uncommon to read about, on an internet forum, homeowners who have hastily decided to install a geo-system in October or November without having done any research. They are often the ones who post messages several months later indicating that their lack of knowledge resulted in making some poor choices. Often, they claim that the wrong size heat pump or loop field was installed. One forum poster in particular comes to mind. He stated that after a light snowfall, his front yard was the only property on his street that was snow-covered. The area was above his ground loops. Clearly, this was the result of poor loop design. Whether the loops were undersized, too close together, not buried deep enough or a combination of these conditions, this could have been avoided. The shortage of highly experienced HVAC personnel in the geothermal field mandates that the homeowner take the time to absorb as much information as he can about these systems. If he does, the reward will be a heating and cooling system that requires minimum maintenance and results in low monthly electric bills.

Third, if the geo-system would be a retro-installation and the homeowner currently uses natural gas for heating, a preliminary design heat load estimation can be performed by the homeowner as described in an earlier chapter. This involves obtaining daily readings of the natural gas meter during the coldest period of the winter. The homeowner's calculated heating load estimate can then be compared to that of the bidding installers. This would help to weed out heating/cooling bids that specified a system that was too large or too small.

Flowchart 1 lists the tasks the homeowner should accomplish prior to meeting with an installer.

Flowchart 2 identifies the installer issues that the homeowner should focus on when he initially meets a prospective installer/contractor. The bidder should be able to answer the questions on this chart prior to a proposal being completed and sent to the homeowner.

Flowcharts 3 to 8 can be used to evaluate the detailed proposals received from system installers to clarify the details of the installation including cost and warrantees. The information in these flowcharts should be used to make sure that the contract contains all relevant details.

The internet has many forums which the homeowner should take advantage of to become better informed about geothermal systems. The following websites offer active discussions on the installation and maintenance of residential geothermal systems:

https://www.greenbuildingtalk.com/Forums.aspx

http://hvac-talk.com

http://forum.geoexchange.org

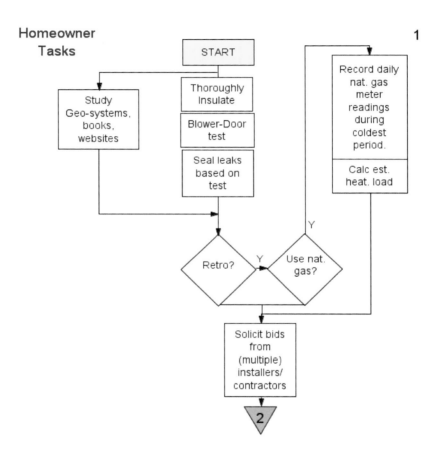

Homeowner Tasks

START

Study Geo-systems, books, websites

Thoroughly Insulate

Blower-Door test

Seal leaks based on test

Record daily nat. gas meter readings during coldest period.

Calc est. heat. load

Retro?

Y

Use nat. gas?

Y

1

Solicit bids from (multiple) installers/ contractors

2

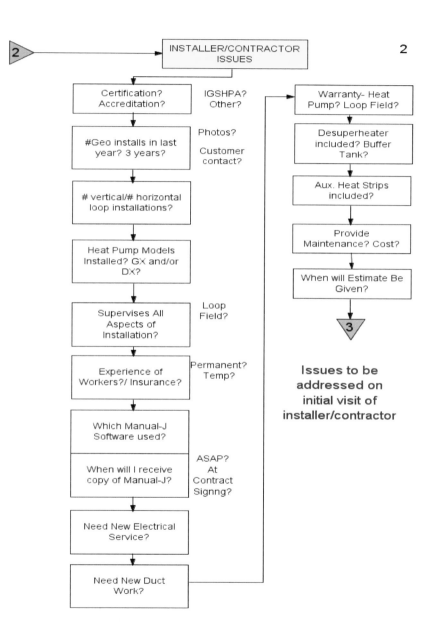

2 → INSTALLER/CONTRACTOR ISSUES   2

Certification? Accreditation?   IGSHPA? Other?

Warranty- Heat Pump? Loop Field?

#Geo installs in last year? 3 years?   Photos? Customer contact?

Desuperheater included? Buffer Tank?

vertical/# horizontal loop installations?

Aux. Heat Strips included?

Heat Pump Models Installed? GX and/or DX?

Provide Maintenance? Cost?

Supervises All Aspects of Installation?   Loop Field?

When will Estimate Be Given?

Experience of Workers?/ Insurance?   Permanent? Temp?

3

Which Manual-J Software used?

When will I receive copy of Manual-J?   ASAP? At Contract Signng?

Issues to be addressed on initial visit of installer/contractor

Need New Electrical Service?

Need New Duct Work?

172

3   3

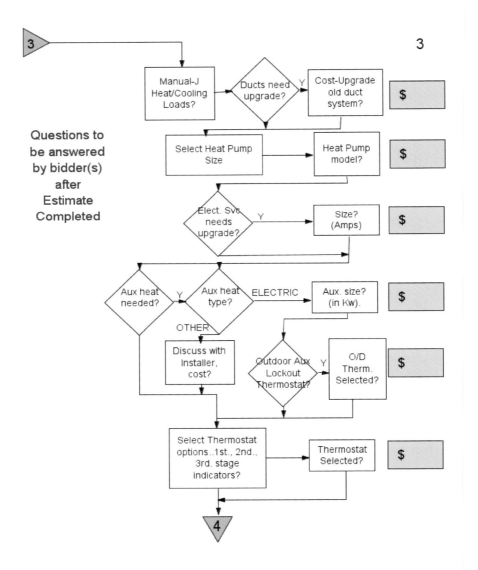

Questions to be answered by bidder(s) after Estimate Completed

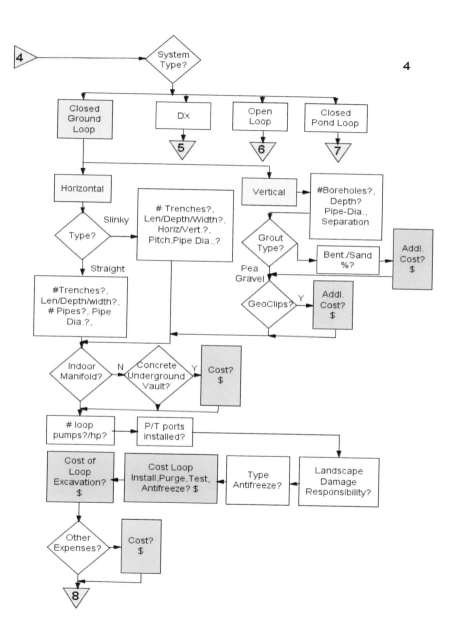

4

4 → System Type?

System Type? →
- Closed Ground Loop
- DX → **5**
- Open Loop → **6**
- Closed Pond Loop → **7**

Closed Ground Loop →
- Horizontal → Type?
  - Slinky → # Trenches?, Len/Depth/Width?, Horiz/Vert.?, Pitch, Pipe Dia.,?
  - Straight → #Trenches?, Len/Depth/width?, # Pipes?, Pipe Dia.?,
- Vertical → #Boreholes?, Depth? Pipe-Dia., Separation

Vertical → Grout Type?
- Bent./Sand %? → Addl. Cost? $
- Pea Gravel
- GeoClips? — Y → Addl. Cost? $

Indoor Manifold? — N → Concrete Underground Vault? — Y → Cost? $

loop pumps?/hp? → P/T ports installed?

P/T ports installed? → Landscape Damage Responsibility? → Type Antifreeze? → Cost Loop Install, Purge, Test, Antifreeze? $ → Cost of Loop Excavation? $

Cost of Loop Excavation? $ → Other Expenses?
- Cost? $
- → **8**

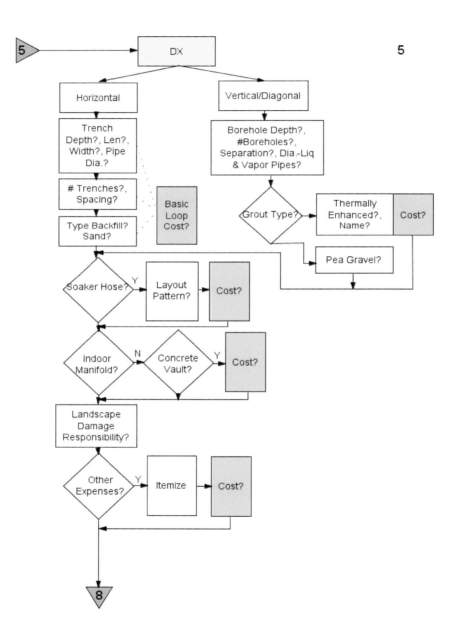

5

DX

Horizontal

Trench Depth?, Len?, Width?, Pipe Dia.?

Trenches?, Spacing?

Type Backfill? Sand?

Basic Loop Cost?

Vertical/Diagonal

Borehole Depth?, #Boreholes?, Separation?, Dia.-Liq & Vapor Pipes?

Grout Type?

Thermally Enhanced?, Name?

Cost?

Pea Gravel?

Soaker Hose? Y Layout Pattern? Cost?

Indoor Manifold? N Concrete Vault? Y Cost?

Landscape Damage Responsibility?

Other Expenses? Y Itemize Cost?

8

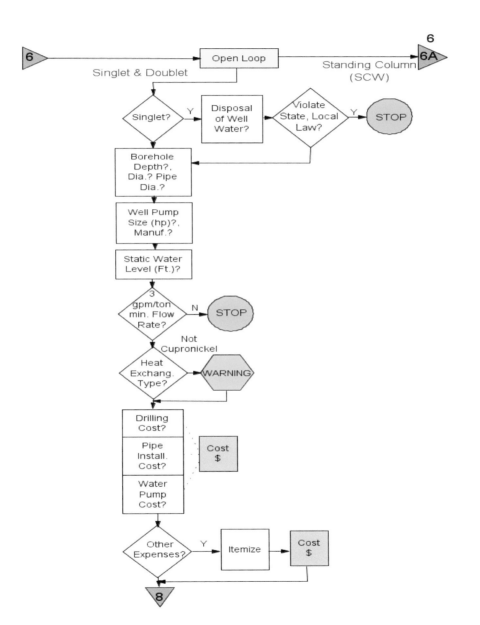

6 ▶

Singlet & Doublet

Open Loop

6
6A ▶

Standing Column (SCW)

Singlet? — Y → Disposal of Well Water? → Violate State, Local Law? — Y → STOP

Borehole Depth?, Dia.? Pipe Dia.?

Well Pump Size (hp)?, Manuf.?

Static Water Level (Ft.)?

3 gpm/ton min. Flow Rate? — N → STOP

Not Cupronickel

Heat Exchang. Type? → WARNING

Drilling Cost?

Pipe Install. Cost?

Water Pump Cost?

Cost $

Other Expenses? — Y → Itemize → Cost $

8

176

7

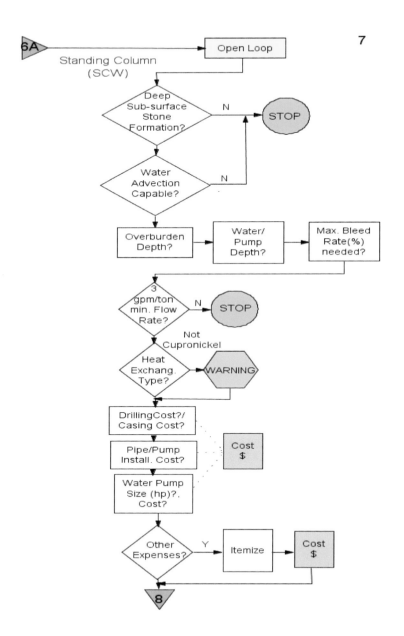

8

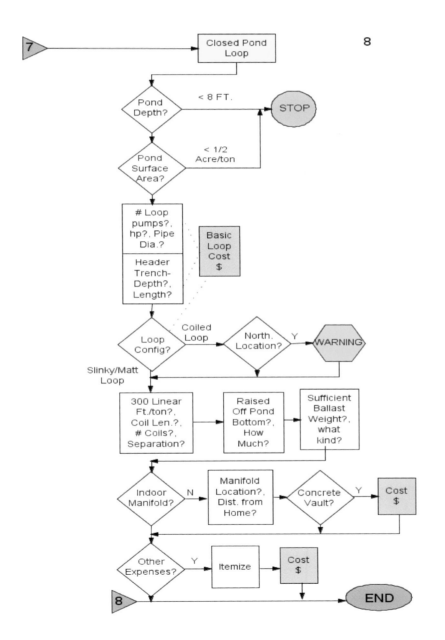

APPENDIX A

AVERAGE ANNUAL GROUND TEMPERATURES (degrees F.)

UNITED STATES

Alabama	Birmingham 65	Mobile 70	Montgomery 67		
Alaska	Anchorage 40	Fairbanks 32			
Arizona	Phoenix 73				
Arkansas	Little Rock 64				
California	Fresno 68	Los Angeles 64	Sacramento 67	San Diego 64	San Francisco 60
Colorado	Denver 52				
Connecticut	Hartford 51				
Delaware	Dover 57				
Florida	Daytona Beach 70	Jacksonville 71	Miami 78	Tallahassee 69	Tampa 75
Georgia	Atlanta 62	Savannah 67			
Hawaii	Honolulu 79				
Idaho	Boise 47				
Illinois	Chicago 51	Springfield 56			
Indiana	Fort Wayne 53	Indianapolis 55			
Iowa	Des Moines 53				
Kansas	Wichita 59				
Ohio	Cincinatti 57				
Kentucky	Lexington 60	Louisville 60			
Louisiana	New Orleans 70	Shreveport 66			
Maine	Caribou 46	Portland 48			
Maryland	Baltimore 57				
Massachusetts	Boston 50	Worchester 50			

Michigan	Detroit 50	Flint 49	Grand Rapids 46	
Minnesota	Duluth 41	Minneapolis 47		
Mississippi	Jackson 67			
Missouri	Kansas City 58	St. Louis 58		
Montana	Billings 49	Helena 47		
Nebraska	Omaha 53			
Nevada	Las Vegas 69	Reno 50		
New Hampshire	Concord 50			
New Jersey	Trenton 55			
New Mexico	Albuquerque 59			
New York	Albany 50	Buffalo 50	New York City 52	
North Carolina	Asheville 59	Charlotte 62	Greensboro 60	Raleigh 62
North Dakota	Bismarck 44	Fargo 42		
Ohio	Cleveland 51	Colombus 55	Dayton 50	
Oklahoma	Oklahoma City 62			
Oregon	Portland 54			
Pennsylvania	Harrisburg 52	Philadelphia 55	Pittsburgh 52	
South Carolina	Charleston 66	Columbia 64	Greenville 62	
South Dakota	Sioux Falls 51			
Tennessee	Knoxville 61	Memphis 63	Nashville 60	
Texas	Austin 71	Dallas 68	Houston 71	San Antonio 72
Utah	Salt Lake City 53			
Vermont	Burlington 46			
Virginia	Norfolk 61	Richmond 60	Roanoke 59	
DC	Washington 57			

Washington	Seattle 53	Spokane 49			
West Virginia	Charleston 58				
Wisconsin	La Crosse 48	Milwaukee 47			
Wyoming	Cheyenne 48				

CANADA

Calgary 42	Edmonton 40	Vancouver 53	Winnipeg 40	Moncton 42	Saint John's 43
Halifax 45	Ottawa 45	Toronto 48	Charlottetown 42	Montreal 46	Regina 39

AUSTRALIA

Adelaide 64	Brisbane 72	Canberra 67	Melbourne 59	Perth 67	Sydney 67

EUROPE

Austria	Salzburg 51	Vienna 50			
Belgium	Brussels 52				
Bulgaria	Sofia	55			
Czech Republic	Prague 50				
Denmark	Copenhagen 47				
France	Bordeaux 61	Lyon 57	Marseille 59	Nantes 56	Paris 54
Germany	Berlin 52	Frankfurt 52	Munich 49	Stuttgart 51	
Hungary	Budapest 53				
Ireland	Dublin	52			
Italy	Milan 57	Naples 63	Rome 61	Venice 58	
Poland	Krakow 48	Warsaw 49			
Romania	Bucharest 54				
Spain	Barcelona 62	Madrid 60	Sevilla 67	Valencia 65	
Sweden	Stockholm 47				
Switzerland	Geneva 53				
Yugoslavia	Belgrade 55				

APPENDIX B   HEAT CAPACITIES OF VARIOUS SUBSTANCES   (Specific Heat)

Substance	BTU/lb degree F.	KJ/kg degree K.
Ashes	.20	.84
Asphalt	.22	.92
Basalt rock	.20	.84
Brick (common)	.22	.92
Cement (dry)	.37	1.55
Charcoal	.24	1.0
Clay (sandy)	.33	1.38
Coal (anthracite)	.30	1.26
Coal (bituminous)	.33	1.38
Concrete (light)	.23	.96
Dolomite rock	.22	.92
Earth (dry)	.30	1.26
Granite	.19	.79
Gypsum	.26	1.09
Ice	.50	2.09
Limestone	.20	.84
Marble	.21	.88
Mud (wet)	.60	2.51
Peat	.45	1.88
Plaster (light)	.24	1.0
Rock Salt	.22	.92
Sand	.19	.80
Sand (quartz)	.19	.80
Sandstone	.22	.92
Serpentine	.26	1.09
Water (pure)	1.0	4.19

APPENDIX C   HEAT PUMP MANUFACTURERS

The following heat pump brands/manufacturers are listed in alphabetic order. No endorsement for a particular one is being made.

DX Systems (which use a refrigerant-based loop field)

BRAND/MANUFACTURER	WEB ADDRESS
Avenir Energie (DANFOSS GROUP)	avenir-energie.com
EarthLinked	earthlinked.com
ETA (Earth To Air Systems, LLC)	earthtoair.com
Nordic (Maritime Geothermal Ltd.)	nordicghp.com
SOFATH (Termatis Technologies SAS)	sofath.com

Split Systems (Air controller in a separate, remote unit)

BRAND/MANUFACTURER	WEB ADDRESS
Carrier (United Technologies)	residential.carrier.com
Century (Heat Controller)	century-hvac.com
ClimateMaster (LSB Industries)	climatemaster.com
Comfort Aire (Heat Controller)	comfortaire-hvac.com
Florida Heat Pump (Bosch Group)	fhp-mfg.com
GeoComfort (Enertech Manufacturing LLC)	geocomfort.com
HydroHeat (Hydro Delta Corp.)	hydrodelta.com
Hydron Module (Enertech Manufacturing LLC.)	hydronmodule.com
WaterFurnace	waterfurnace.com

Packaged Units (All components in one cabinet)

BRAND/MANUFACTURER	WEB ADDRESS
Bard	bardhvac.com
Boreal	boreal-geothermal.com
Carrier (United Technologies)	residential.carrier.com
Century (Heat Controller)	century-hvac.com
ClimateMaster (LSB Industries)	climatemaster.com
Comfort Aire (Heat Controller)	comfortaire-hvac.com
Fedders (Airwell Group)	fedders.com
Florida Heat Pump (Bosch Group)	fhp-mfg.com
GeoComfort (Enertech Manufacturing LLC)	geocomfort.com
GeoSource (Econar Energy Systems Corp.)	econar.com
HydroHeat (Hydro Delta Corp.)	hydrodelta.com
Hydron Module (Enertech Manufacturing LLC.)	hydronmodule.com
Hydro Temp	hydro-temp.com
Klimaire	klimaire.com
Nordic (Maritime Geothermal LTD.)	Nordicghp.com
Northern Heat Pump	northernheatpump.com
Polar Bear Energy	polarbearenergy.com
Sakura	sakura-aircon.com
Sofath (Termatis Technologies)	sofath.com
TILI	tili-northamerica.com
WaterFurnace	waterfurnace.com

LaVergne, TN USA
16 January 2011
212472LV00004B